THE CHARTER

OF THE

City of East Saginaw,

AS ENACTED AND AMENDED BY THE

LEGISLATURE OF THE STATE OF MICHIGAN,

TOGETHER WITH OTHER

ACTS OF THE LEGISLATURE,

FOR THE USE OF THE

OFFICERS OF THE CITY.

COMPILED AND PRINTED BY ORDER OF THE COMMON COUNCIL.

EAST SAGINAW:
ENTERPRISE PRINTING COMPANY, WASHINGTON STREET,
1869.

CHARTER
OF THE
CITY OF EAST SAGINAW.

An Act to Incorporate the City of East Saginaw, Approved Feb. 14th, 1859, with Amendments made thereto by the Acts Approved March 1st, 1865; March 22d, 1867, and March 16th, 1869.

TITLE I.

INCORPORATION—CITY AND WARD BOUNDARIES.

TITLE I.

(§ 1.) SECTION 1. *The People of the State of Michigan enact:* That so much of the township of Buena Vista, in the County of Saginaw, as is embraced in the following boundaries, to-wit: commencing at a point in the centre of Saginaw river, where the north section line of said section eighteen, in township twelve north, of range five east, crosses said river; thence east along said section line to the north-east corner of said section eighteen; thence south along the east section lines of sections eighteen, nineteen and thirty to the south-east corner of said section thirty, in said township and range; thence west along the south line of said section thirty to the south-west corner of said section thirty; thence north on the west section line of said section thirty, to the south-east corner of the James Riley Reservation; thence west along the south line of said James Riley Reservation * to the centre of Saginaw River, thence down Saginaw River to the place of beginning, be and the

Boundaries of the City.

* Amended by Act of 1869, so as to run to east line of Mackinaw road, thence north to east line of the bayou, thence along the east line of bayou to its junction with the river, thence down the centre of river, &c. That portion west of bayou is attached to town of Spaulding.

same is hereby detached and set off from said township and constituted an incorporated City by name of the City of East Saginaw, and by that name may sue and be sued, implead and be impleaded, complain and defend, in any court of record, and any other place whatsoever; may have a common seal and alter it at pleasure; and may take, hold, purchase, lease, convey and dispose of, any real, personal or mixed estate for the use of said corporation. [*Act of* 1865.]

Incorporation. Seal. Hold Property.

(§ 2.) SECTION 2. Said City shall be divided into six Wards, as follows: All that part of the City lying north of the centre of Miller street, shall constitute the First Ward; all that part of the City lying between the centre of Miller street and the centre of Johnson street, shall constitute the Second Ward; all that portion of the City lying between the centre of Johnson street and the centre of William street, to its junction with Genesee street, thence along the centre of Genesee street to the centre line of Janes street, thence along the centre line of Janes street to the East City line, shall constitute the Third Ward; all that portion of the City lying between the line last mentioned and the centre line of Hoyt street, to where said line shall intersect the centre line of Walnut street, thence along the centre line of Walnut street to the east City line, shall constitute the Fourth Ward; all that part of the City lying South of the centre line of Hoyt street and west of the centre line of Maple street, including its intersection with Martha street, and as extended on the township line to the south City line, shall constitute the Fifth Ward; all that portion of said City lying east of the above boundary line of the Fifth Ward, and south of the above boundary line of the Fourth Ward, shall constitute the Sixth Ward of said City. [*Act of* 1869.]

First. Second. Third. Fourth. Fifth. Sixth.

TITLE II.

OFFICERS:—WHO ELECTED; WHO APPOINTED; QUALIFICATIONS; OATH; TERMS; REMOVAL; VACANCY; ELECTIONS, HOW CONDUCTED.

(§ 3.) SECTION 1. The following officers of the City of East Saginaw shall be elected at the annual City election, by the qualified electors of the whole City, voting in their respective Wards on a general ticket, viz: one Mayor, one Recorder, one Treasurer, and one Director of the Poor. *City Officers.*

The following officers of the corporation shall be elected at said election, on a Ward ticket, in each Ward, by the qualified electors *Ward Officers.*

thereof, viz: two Aldermen, two School Inspectors, one Supervisor, one Collector (of taxes,) and one Constable.

Officers to be elected by the Council by ballot.

The following officers of said corporation shall be chosen by the Common Council, as hereinafter provided, by ballot, viz: one City Clerk, one Controller, one Assessor, one Marshal, one Street Commissioner, one City Surveyor, one City Attorney, one City Physician, two Cemetery Commissioners, and one Chief Engineer of the Fire Department.

Officers to be appointed by the Council.

The following officers of said corporation shall be appointed by the Common Council, in such manner as is hereinafter provided, or as the said Common Council may, by ordinance, direct, viz: an assistant Marshal, one or more keepers of the City Prison, Almshouse or Hospital, two assistant Engineers of the Fire Department, Pound Masters, Sealers of Weights and Measures, Board of Sewer Commissioners, Board of Water Commissioners, Inspectors of Gas and Gas Meters, Clerks of Markets and for City Officers, Inspectors of Fire-Wood, Hay and Provisions, Harbor Masters, Port Wardens, Fire Wardens, Scavengers, Common Criers, Auctioneers, Weigh Masters, and such other officers as may be necessary to carry into effect the powers herein granted.

Council to regulate and prescribe compensation.

The said Common Council shall have power to regulate and prescribe the duties of all officers of said corporation, appointed by virtue of the powers herein granted, and to fix the fees, compensation and emoluments to be paid such officers, except as herein otherwise provided. [*Act of* 1869.]

Officers must reside in City and Ward.

(§ 4.) SEC. 2. No person shall be eligible to either of said elective offices, unless he shall then be an elector and resident of said City, nor shall he be eligible to any such office for any Ward or district, unless he shall then be an elector and resident of such Ward or district, and when any officer elected or appointed for any Ward or district, shall cease to reside in said City, or if elected or appointed for any Ward or district, shall cease to reside in such Ward or district, his office shall thereby become vacant. [*Act of* 1859.]

Removals will vacate

Time and notice of annual election.

(§ 5.) SEC. 3. An election shall be held in each Ward, in the year 1865, on the 10th day of March, and annually thereafter on the first Monday in April in each year, at such place as the Common Council shall appoint by a notice published at least six days previous to the election, in a newspaper printed in said City, or by posting printed notices of the holding of said election, in at least three of the most public places in each Ward, at least six days previous to said election. *Provided:* That for the annual election in the year 1865, the notice to be given as hereinbefore provided, may be, by a notice of four days given in the manner in this section provided, if sufficient time shall not elapse after the passage of this act for the usual six days notice. [*Act of* 1865.]

(§ 6.) SEC. 4. At the first annual election after the passage of this act, there shall be elected, by the qualified electors of said City, voting in their respective Wards, four Justices of the Peace, one of whom shall be elected for the term of one year, one for the term of two years, one for the term of three years, and one for the term of four years; and the term for which each person is voted shall be distinguished on the ballots, who shall enter upon the duties of the office immediately upon being qualified according to law; and at every annual election thereafter, there shall be elected one justice of the peace, who shall hold his office for the term of four years; and every Justice of the Peace elected in said City shall take the oath and file his bond within ten days after his election, and enter upon the performance of the duties of his office on the tenth day after his election; and in case of vacancy in said office of Justice of the Peace, the same shall be filled at the succeeding annual election, as provided by law. [*Act of* 1859.] **Justices of the Peace.**

There shall also be elected by the qualified electors of said City, voting in their respective Wards, one Mayor, one Treasurer and one Director of the Poor, who shall hold their office for one year, or until their successors are elected and qualified. At the annual election in said city, in the year 1870, and every two years thereafter, there shall be elected, by the qualified electors of said City, voting in their respective Wards, one Recorder, who shall hold his office for two years, or until his successor shall be elected and qualified. At the annual election to be held in said City, in the year 1869, there shall be elected, by the qualified electors thereof, two Aldermen for each Ward, one for the term of one year and one for the term of two years; and thereafter, there shall be elected annually, in each Ward, one Alderman for the term of two years. At the annual election, in the year 1869, there shall also be elected **Mayor, Treasurer, Director of Poor.** **Recorder.**

School Inspectors. by the qualified electors thereof, in each Ward, two School Inspectors, one for the term of one year and one for the term of two years, and thereafter there shall be elected, annually, in each Ward one School Inspector, for the term of two years. There shall also be elected, annually, in each Ward, by the qualified electors thereof, Constables. one Constable, who shall give like security, perform all the duties, be vested with like powers and be subject, in all respects, to the laws of the State, as provided in the case of Constables in the the townships of this State. There shall also be elected, at the annual election held in said city, in the year 1869, in each Ward, by Supervisors the qualified electors thereof, one Supervisor, who shall hold office as follows:—those elected for the even numbered Wards, for one year, those for the odd numbered Wards, for two years, and there-Term of office. after, upon the expiration of such terms, their successors shall be elected for two years, in each Ward: *Provided*, That in case of Vacancy. vacancy, the Common Council shall have power to fill such vacancy by appointment, such appointee to hold office until the next annual election, when such vacancy shall be filled by the electors of the Ward in which such vacancy shall have occurred: Said Supervi-Duties and compensation of Supervisors. sors shall be entitled to the same compensation, and shall be paid in the same manner, and perform all the duties of Supervisors of townships, as provided by law, in their several Wards, except such duties as are by this act devolved upon the Assessor or other officer of said City; and the Supervisors shall, in addition to the foregoing compensation, receive three dollars per day, for every day actually engaged in the duties of their office, to be paid by the City.[a] There shall also be elected, at the annual election, in each Ward of said Collector of Taxes. City, by the qualified electors thereof, one Collector of Taxes, who shall become duly qualified, give the same bonds, and be vested, in Powers and duties of. all respects, with the same powers as are by the laws of this State conferred upon the Treasurers of townships, for the collection of taxes for County and State purposes, and each of said collectors shall also give such bonds, with sureties, as may be required by the Common Council, for the faithful performance of all duties devolved upon them by this act, or by any ordinance of said City, and they shall possess the same powers, for the collection of City taxes, as is conferred upon township Treasurers of this State, for the collection

[a] *Vide* Sec. 11, of Title 2; Sec. 6, of Title 4, and Sec. 6, of Title 5.

of taxes in the townships of this State, or may hereafter be conferred by law. [*Act of* 1869.]

Council shall elect Marshal, Clerk, Physician, Street Commis'ner, Surveyor, Chief Engineer.

(§ 7.) SEC. 5. The Common Council shall at the third regular meeting in the month of April in each year, or as soon thereafter as may be, and as often as any vacancy occurs in any of the offices in this section named, appoint, by ballot one City Marshal, one Clerk of said city, one City Physician, one City Surveyor, one Street Commissioner, and one Chief Engineer of Fire department, to hold their respective offices for one year, or during the pleasure of the Common Council. Cem. Com. They shall also appoint two Commissioners for the City Cemetery or Cemeteries, one of whom shall hold his office for the term of two years, and one of them for the term of one year; and annually thereafter, the said Common Council shall appoint one Commissioner of the City Cemetery, who shall hold his office for two years. City Attorney. They shall also appoint one City Attorney to act as Attorney and Counselor at law for said city, who shall hold office for one year, or during the pleasure of the Common Council, and who shall receive an annual salary to be fixed by the Common Council, and who shall not receive for any duties imposed or services rendered to said city during the term of his office, besides his salary, any fee or reward whatever, which shall be paid out of or withheld from the treasury of said city. Appoint one Ass't Marshal. Police and Watchmen. The Common Council may, from time to time, as may be necessary, appoint an Assistant Marshal, one Captain of the Watche and so many Police Constables and Watchmen as they may deem, expedient or necessary to preserve the peace of said city and protect the property of the citizens, and may make all necessary rules and regulations for the appointment and government of said Police Constables and Watchmen, not herein provided for, and said Police Constables and Watchmen shall have the same power and authority Powers of to make complaints and arrests, as constables now have by law, except as to the service and return of civil process and proceedings in civil cases, and shall be subject to the same liabilities and penalties, except as herein otherwise provided: Proviso. *Provided*, The Common Council may limit or prescribe the duties and powers of such Police Constables and Watchmen by ordinance, and remove them or provide for their suspension or discharge at any time. Other Officers to be appointed. The Common Council shall also appoint a Keeper of the City Prison or Prisons, Work-House, Almshouse, Hospital and so many Fire Wardens, Inspectors of Gas and Gas Metres, Common Criers, Clerks of City Markets, or for City Officers, Inspectors of Firewood, Hay and Provisions, Pound Masters, Sealers of Weights and Measures, Weigh Masters, Auctioneers, Scavengers, and such other officers or boards of officers, as are herein provided for, or which may be created by the ordinances of said city, made pursuant to the provisions of this charter, and such appointments shall be made in such manner as the said Common Council shall authorize and direct, and all such appointees shall hold their offices during the pleasure of said Common Council. [*Act of* 1869.]

Terms of office.

Vacancies provided for

(§ 8.) SEC. 6. When any vacancy occurs in any of the offices which are appointed by the Common Council, either by death, resignation or removal of the incumbent, the said Council may fill such vacancies by appointment for the remainder of the unexpired term for which such officer was appointed. [*Act of* 1859.]

What officers may be removed and how.

(§ 9.) SEC. 7. All officers appointed by the Common Council, by virtue of the powers conferred by this act, may each be removed from office by the Common Council for incompetence, for official misconduct, or for the unfaithful and insufficient performance of the duties of his office, or for disobedience of the ordinances of the Common Council, or for performing any unlawful act: *Provided*, No officer who is required to be elected by ballot, or who is required by this act or by the Common Council to give bonds, shall be removed without reasonable notice of the charges against him, and an opportunity to be heard in his defense, in person and by counsel, nor without a majority of all the members elected to the Common Council, shall, after such notice and hearing, vote for such removal. [*Act of* 1869.]

Mayor may appoint Police, &c.

(§ 10.) SEC. 8. The Mayor may appoint an additional number of Police Constables or Watchmen, not exceeding ten of each, when he shall deem it necessary for the purposes of justice, for the preservation of peace, or for the security of the said city; but no such appointment shall be valid for a longer period than until the next meeting of the Common Council. [*Act of* 1859.]

Polls of election.

(§ 11.) SEC. 9. On the day of election, held by virtue of this act, the polls shall be opened in each ward, at the several places designated by the Common Council, at nine o'clock in the morning, and shall be kept open, without intermission or adjournment, until four o'clock in the afternoon, at which hour they shall be finally closed. [*Act of* 1859.]

(§ 12.) SEC. 10. The inhabitants of the said city, being electors under the constitution of the State of Michigan, and no others, are declared to be electors under this act, and qualified to vote at the elections held by virtue of this act; and each person offering to vote at any such election, if challenged by an elector of said city, before his vote shall be received, shall take one of the oaths now provided by the laws of this State, entitled "an Act to provide for holding General and Special Elections," unless such person shall claim to be an elector under the proviso named in Section thirty of this title, and in that case the oath shall be varied according to that proviso, which oath shall be administered to him by one of the Inspectors of election, and if any person shall swear falsely, upon conviction thereof, he shall be liable to the pains and penalties of perjury, but the Common Council of said city are hereby authorized and empowered to provide by general ordinance, from time to time, to so change the form of the oath or oaths to be administered to such elector (if challenged) as to conform to the constitution and laws of the State which may from time [to time] be in force. [*Act of* 1865.]

Electors. Challenges. Oath. Penalty.

(§ 13.) SEC. 11. The Supervisors and Aldermen of each Ward shall constitute the Board of Inspectors of elections, two of whom shall constitute a quorum, and such one of their number as they may appoint, shall be chairman of said board; the board shall also appoint two competent persons to be clerks of the elections, who shall take the oath of office required by law; and each of said Board of Inspectors shall be authorized to administer any oaths required by law to be taken by either of said Inspectors, Clerks, or other persons at said elections. [*Act of* 1869.]

Inspectors and Clerks of election.

(§ 14.) SEC. 12. Inspectors of elections, as specified in the preceding Section, shall be Inspectors of election held in said Wards respectively, as well as for election of State, District and County, as for the City and Ward Officers. [*Act of* 1859.]

(§ 15.) SEC. 13. The Electors shall vote by ballot, and each person offering to vote shall deliver his ballot, so folded as to conceal its contents, to one of the Inspectors, in the presence of the

Vote by ballot, &c.

Board; the ballot shall be a paper ticket, which shall contain, written or printed, or partly written and partly printed, the names of the persons for whom the elector intends to vote, and shall designate the office to which each person so named or intended by him to be chosen; but no ballot shall contain a greater number of names of persons, designated for any office than there are persons to be chosen at the election to fill such office. On the outside of each ballot, when folded, there shall appear, written or printed, one of the following words, "ward," "city;" but no ballot found in the proper box, shall be rejected for want of such endorsement. [*Act of* 1859.]

Ballots and boxes. (§ 16.) SEC. 14. The ballot endorsed "city" shall contain the names of persons designated as officers for the city; the ballot containing the names of persons designated as officers for a ward, shall be endorsed "ward." The Common Council shall provide two boxes for each ward, with locks and keys, in which these two kinds of votes shall be deposited separately. [*Act of* 1859.]

Ballots for vacancies. (§ 17.) SEC. 15. If, at any annual election to be held in the said city, there shall be one or more vacancies to be supplied in any office, and at the same time any person is to be elected for the full term of said office, the term for which each person is voted for, for the said office, shall be designated on the ballot. [*Act of* 1859.]

Canvas of votes. (§ 18.) SEC. 16. Immediately after the closing of the polls, the Inspectors of election shall forthwith, without adjournment, publicly canvass the votes received by them, and declare the result; and shall on the same, or on the next day, make a certificate, stating the number of votes given for each person for each office, and shall file such statement and certificate, on the day of election, or on the next day, with the clerk of the city. [*Act of* 1859.]

Duties of Inspecters. (§ 19.) SEC. 17. It shall be the duty of the Inspectors of election, on receiving the vote, as specified in Section thirteen of this title, to cause the same, without being opened or inspected, to be deposited in the proper box provided by the Common Council for that purpose; the said Board shall also write down, or cause to be written down, the name of each elector voting at such election, in a poll list to be kept by said Inspectors of election, or under their direction. [*Act of* 1859.]

How Inspectors shall canvas. (§ 20.) SEC. 18. The manner of canvassing said votes shall be as follows: The Inspectors shall proceed first to count the ballots unopened, in the box marked "city," and if the number of ballots so counted shall exceed the number of names of electors contained in the poll list, one of the Inspectors shall draw out and destroy as many as the number of ballots exceeds the number of electors contained in said poll list; and if two or more ballots are found rolled or folded up together, they shall not be counted; and they shall proceed in the same manner with the ballots contained in the box marked "ward," they shall then proceed to count and estimate said votes as provided in the preceding Section: *Provided*, That at the first election to be held under this act, the electors may choose in each Ward three competent proper persons to act as a Board of Inspectors of election, who shall each take the constitutional oath of office before they enter on the performance of their duties: *And also provided*, That at said first election the polls shall be opened at such place in each Ward as the present Common Council of the Village of East Saginaw shall appoint, of which place public notice shall be given by said Village Council at least six days prior to such election: *And provided further*, That the Inspectors of said first election shall certify the statement and certificate mentioned in Section sixteen of this title to the present Recorder of the said Village of East Saginaw, and the Common Council of said Village, for the purpose of determining the result of said first election is hereby vested with all the powers hereby conferred on the Common Council of the City by Section nineteen and twenty of this title. [*Act of* 1859.] Proviso.

(§ 21.) SEC. 19. The person receiving the greatest number of votes for any office in said City or Ward, shall be deemed to have been duly elected to such office; and if any officer, shall not have been chosen by reason of two or more candidates having received an equal number of votes for the same office, the Common Council shall take as many strips of paper of equal size, as there are persons having an equal number of such votes, and write a ballot for each of such persons, one on each of said slips of paper, and shall put said ballots together in a hat or box, and one of the members of the Common Council shall then draw from said hat one of said ballots, and the person whose name shall be upon the ballot so drawn shall be declared elected. [*Act of* 1859.] Who shall be deemed elected. Tie-vote, how determined.

(§ 22.) SEC. 20. The Common Council of the preceding year shall convene on the Wednesday next succeeding such election, at Canvas by the council.

two o'clock in the afternoon, at their usual place of meeting; and the statement of votes filed with the Clerk of the City, by the Inspectors of election, shall be produced by said Clerk, when the Common Council shall forthwith determine and certify, in the manner provided by law, what persons are duly elected, at the said election to the several offices respectively. Such certificate shall be made in duplicate, one of which shall be filed with the Clerk of the City, and the other with the Clerk of the County of Saginaw. All officers elected as hereinbefore provided, shall enter upon the duties of their respective offices on the tenth day next following such election, unless otherwise herein provided. [*Act of* 1859.]

Certificate, how made and filed.

Clerk to notify. Oaths, &c.

(§ 23.) SEC. 21. It shall be the duty of the Clerk of said City, as soon as practicable, and within two days after the meeting of the Common Council, as provided in the preceding Section, to notify the officers, respectively, of their election; and the said officers, so elected and notified, as aforesaid, shall within ten days after such election, take the oath of office prescribed by the constitution of this State, before some officer authorized by law to administer oaths, and file the same with the Clerk of the City. [*Act of* 1859.]

Vacancy in case of an Alderman.

(§ 24.) SEC. 22. Whenever a vacancy occurs in the office of Alderman, by his refusal or neglect to take the oath of office, within the time required by this act, by his resignation, death, ceasing to be an inhabitant of the City or Ward for which he shall have been elected, removal from office, or by the decision of a competent tribunal declaring void his election, or for any other cause, the Common Council of said City shall immediately appoint a Special election to be held in the Ward for which such officer was chosen, at some suitable place therein, not less than five days nor more than fifteen days from the time of such appointment: *Provided*, That in case any such vacancy shall occur in the said office of Alderman within three months before the first Monday of March in any year, it shall be optional with the Common Council to order a Special election or not, as they shall deem expedient. [*Act of* 1859.]

Vacancies, except Alderman and Justice of the Peace.

(§ 25.) SEC. 23. In case a vacancy shall occur in any of the offices in this act declared to be elective or appointive, except Alderman and Justices of the Peace, the Common Council may, in their discretion, fill such vacancy by the appointment of a suitable person, who is an elector, and if appointed for a ward, who is also a resident of the Ward for which he shall be appointed, and any officer appointed to fill a vacancy, if the office is elective, shall hold by virtue of such appointment only until the tenth day after the election next succeeding; if an elective office which shall have become vacant was of that class whose terms of office continue after the next annual election, a successor for the unexpired term shall be elected at the next annual election. [*Act of* 1859.]

(§ 26.) SEC. 24. Whenever a Special Election is to be held, the Common Council shall cause to be delivered to the Inspectors of election in the Ward where such officer is to be chosen, a notice signed by them, specifying the officer to be chosen, and the day and place at which such election is to be held, and the proceedings at such election shall be the same as at the Annual General Election; such notice shall also be published in a newspaper of the City, at least once, or posted in three public places in the City or Ward, as the case may be, before the day of such Special election. [*Act of* 1859.] **Special elections.**

(§ 27.) SEC. 25. Every person chosen or appointed by the Common Council, before he enters upon the duties of his office, and within five days after being notified of his appointment, shall cause to be filed in the office of the City Clerk, a notice in writing, signifying his acceptance of such office. [*Act of* 1859.] **Acceptance to be filed.**

(§ 28.) SEC. 26. If any person, elected or appointed under this title, shall not take and subscribe the oath of office, and file the same as therein directed, or shall not cause a notice of acceptance to be filed as therein directed, or if required by the Common Council to execute an official bond or undertaking, shall neglect to execute and file the same, in the manner and within the time prescribed by the Common Council, such neglect shall be deemed a refusal to serve, unless before any step is taken to fill any such office by another incumbent, such oath shall be taken or such acceptance be signified as aforesaid. [*Act of* 1859.] **Neglect to file acceptance.**

(§ 29.) SEC. 27. At the expiration of twenty days after any election or appointment of any officer or officers in the said City, the Clerk of the said City shall deliver to the Common Council a list of the persons elected or appointed, and of the office to which they are chosen therein, specifying such as have filed with him the **Duty of City Clerk.**

oath of office, or notice of acceptance required by this act, and such as shall have omitted to file the same within the time herein prescribed. [*Act of* 1859.]

Duty of Mayor. (§ 30.) SEC. 28. The Mayor shall report to the Common Council the names of such officers as shall have neglected to give the Bond and security required by the provisions of this Act. [*Act of* 1859.]

Resignation (§ 31.) SEC. 29. Resignations by any officer authorized to be chosen or appointed by this Act, shall be made to the Common Council, subject to their approval and acceptance. [*Act of* 1859.]

Right to vote in ward. (§ 32.) SEC. 30. At all City elections, every elector shall vote in the Ward where he shall have resided ten days next preceding the day of election, otherwise he may vote in the Ward from which he removed: *Provided*, He shall have resided in said Ward ten days prior to such removal. The residence of an elector under this Act shall be the Ward where he boards or takes his regular meals. [*Act of* 1859.]

Vacancy in Inspectors of election. (§ 33.) SEC. 31. At any election held under this Act, if, from any cause, either or all of the Inspectors of election shall fail to attend any such election, at the appointed time and place, his or their place may be supplied for the time being by the electors present, who shall elect any of their number *viva voce*, who when so elected, shall be duly sworn, by an officer authorized to administer oaths, to a faithful performance of their duties. [*Act of* 1859.]

Expenses. (§ 34.) SEC. 32. The expense of any election to be held as provided by this Act, shall be City charges, and defrayed in the same manner as the other contingent expenses of the City. [*Act of* 1859.]

Expiration, Succession to Office. (§ 35.) SEC. 33. Any person elected to any office under this Act, at the expiration of the term thereof, shall continue to hold the same until his successor shall be elected or appointed and qualified; and when a person is elected to fill a vacancy in any elective office, he shall hold the same only during the unexpired portion of the regular term limited to such office, and until his successor shall be elected and qualified. [*Act of* 1859.]

TITLE III.

COMMON COUNCIL:—WHO SHALL CONSTITUTE;—POWERS,—DUTIES,—PROCEEDINGS.

(§ 36.) SEC. 1. The Mayor and Alderman of said City shall constitute the Common Council. They shall meet at such times and places as they shall from time to time appoint; and on special occasions, whenever the Mayor or person officiating as Mayor, (in case of vacancy in the office of the Mayor, or of his absence from the city, or inability to officiate), shall, by written notice appoint, and which shall be served on the members in such a manner

Who constitute Common Council.

Meetings.

and for such time as the Common Council may by ordinance direct. [*Act of* 1859.]

Who to preside.

(§ 37.) SEC. 2. The Mayor, when present, shall preside at the meetings of the Common Council, and in his absence the Recorder shall preside; but if both, Mayor and Recorder be absent, then the Common Council shall appoint one of their number, who shall preside. [*Act of* 1859.]

Power to suspend certain acts lodged in the Mayor.

(§ 38.) SEC. 3. No ordinance or resolution passed by the Common Council, authorizing any public improvement, or for, or concerning the same, or for the payment of money by the Treasurer, shall have any force or effect, if, on the day of its passage, or on the next day thereafter, the Mayor or other officer legally discharging the duties of Mayor, shall lodge in the office of the City Clerk a notice in writing, suspending the immediate operation of such ordinance or resolution. If the Mayor or other officer legally exercising the office of Mayor, shall, within twenty-four hours after the passage of such ordinance or resolution, lodge in the office of the City Clerk his reasons in writing why the same should not go into effect, the same shall not go into effect, nor have any legal operation, unless it shall, at a subsequent meeting of the Common Council, be passed by a majority of two-thirds of all the members of the Common Council then in office, exclusive of the Mayor or other officer legally discharging the duties of Mayor, and if so re-passed, shall go into effect according to the terms thereof. If such reasons in writing shall not be lodged with the Clerk, as above provided, such ordinance or resolution shall have the same operation and effect as if no notice suspending the same had been lodged with the City Clerk, and no ordinance or resolution of the Common Council, for any of the purposes mentioned in this Section, shall go into operation until after the expiration of twenty-four hours after its passage. [*Act of* 1859.]

Clerk to present same to Council.

(§ 39.) SEC. 4. It shall be the duty of the City Clerk to communicate to the Common Council, at the next meeting of the board, any paper that may be lodged with him pursuant to the last preceding Section. [*Act of* 1859.]

Votes of members and how recorded.

(§ 40.) SEC. 5. In all proceedings and meetings of the Common Council, each Alderman present shall, have one vote: *Provided*, Whenever the votes of the Aldermen present shall be equally divided, the Mayor, or when presiding in the absence of the Mayor, the Recorder shall give the casting vote, which vote shall in all cases be entered upon the proceedings of the Council as so decided· [*Act of* 1869.]

(§ 41.) SEC. 6. The sittings of the Common Council shall be public, except when the public interests shall in their opinion require secresy. The minutes of the proceeding shall be kept by the Clerk, and the same shall be open at all times to public inspection. [*Act of* 1859.] Sessions and minutes.

(§ 42.) SEC. 7. The Common Council shall prescribe the rules for the transaction of its business, and for its proceedings, which rules shall have the effect of law, as to the regularity and the recording of said proceedings, and may prescribe in said rules penalties for the non-performance of the duties of Aldermen, City Clerk, or other officers of said Common Council. [*Act of* 1869.] Council to prescribe Rules and penalties.

(§ 43) SEC. 8 A majority of the Aldermen elect shall be a quorum of the Common Council, for the transaction of business. Quorum. In case a quorum shall not attend any regular meeting, any number present less than a quorum may adjourn said meeting to the next regular meeting, or to any time prior to the next regular meeting, and require the Clerk to give notice thereof, as of Special meetings, and such adjournment shall operate to carry with it all business and proceedings postponed to or set down or noticed for such regular meetings, or for any special or adjourned meeting, and no business or proceedings postponed or set down or noticed for any regular, special or adjourned meeting, shall lapse or fail to become invalid, or lose its precedence on the order of business, by reason of a failure to hold such meeting, but the same shall go over, to be acted upon at the next regular adjourned or special meeting. Business shall not lapse for want of a quorum. Shall go over to the next meeting. No public improvement shall be ordered, nor any tax or assessment shall be levied or confirmed, nor any work, services, labor, or material purchased, nor any contract awarded or let, nor any money appropriated to be paid for or out of, or by means of any special assessment or tax, or from the general fund, except by a concurring vote of seven members of the Common Council, including the vote of the Mayor or Recorder when given in case of a tie, when presiding over the sessions of the Council: A vote of seven members required in certain cases. *Provided*, No member of the Council shall be excluded from voting upon any question of improvements, levying assessments or taxes, or on any other proceeding, by reason of his personal or private inter- No member excluded from voting by reason of personal interest, &c.

est in said improvement, assessment, taxes, or any property to be affected by it; nor shall such vote prejudice, void or invalidate any action of the Common Council by reason or on account of any such interest, On all questions ordering any public improvement, levying or confirming any tax, approving any contract, appropriating or expending any moneys, and on the final passage of any ordinance, the names of the members voting for and against the same, by yeas and nays, shall be entered upon the record of proceedings. [*Act of* 1869.]

Vote to be entered on the minutes by ayes and nays.

Aldermen not to be interested in contracts, &c.

(§ 44.) SEC. 9. No member of the Common Council shall, during the period for which he was elected, be appointed to or be competent to hold any office, of which the emoluments are paid from the city treasury, or paid by fees directed to be paid by any act or ordinance of the Common Council, or be directly or indirectly interested in any contract, as principal, surety, or otherwise, the expenses or consideration whereof are to be paid under any ordinance of the Common Council; but this section shall not be construed to prevent the Mayor or Recorder from receiving any salary which may be fixed by the Common Council, nor from holding any office, nor to deprive any Alderman of any emoluments or fees to which he may be entitled by virtue of his office. [*Act of* 1859.]

Gen'l Powers of the Council are enumerated

(§ 45.) SEC. 10. The Common Council in addition to the powers and duties specially conferred upon them in this Act, shall have the management and control of the finances, rights and interests, buildings, and all property, real and personal, belonging to the city, and make such orders and By-Laws relating to the same, as they shall deem proper and necessary; and further they shall have power within said City to enact, make, continue, establish, modify, amend and repeal such Ordinances, By-Laws and Regulations as they deem desirable within said City, for the following purposes:

The Public Peace, &c.

First. To prevent vice and immorality, to preserve public peace and good order, to regulate the Police of the City, to prevent and quell riots, disturbances and disorderly assemblages;

Disorderly and Gaming Houses.

Second. To restrain and prevent disorderly and gaming houses, and houses of ill-fame, all instruments and devices used for gaming, and to prohibit all gaming and fraudulent devices, and regulate or restrain billiard-tables and bowling alleys;

Third. To forbid and prevent the vending or other disposition of liquors and intoxicating drinks, in violation of the laws of this State, and to forbid the selling or giving, to be drank, any intoxicating liquors to any child or young person, without the consent of his or her parent or guardian, and to prohibit, restrain and regulate the sale of all goods, wares and personal property at auction, except in cases of sales authorized by law, and to fix the fees to be paid by and to auctioneers; Intoxicating Liquors. Auctions.

Fourth. To prohibit, restrain, license and regulate all sports, exhibitions of natural or artificial curiosities, caravans of animals, theatrical exhibitions, circuses, or other public performances and exhibitions for money; Exhibitions

Fifth. To abate or remove nuisances of every kind, and to compel the owner or occupant of any grocery, tallow-chandler-shop, butcher's-stall, soap factory, tannery, stable, privy, hog-pen, sewer or other offensive or unwholesome house or place; to cleanse, remove or abate the same, from time to time, as often as they may deem necessary for the health, comfort and convenience of the inhabitants of said city; Abate Nuisances.

Sixth. To direct the location of all slaughter-houses, markets and buildings for storing gunpowder or other combustible substances; Ibid.

Seventh. Concerning the buying, carrying, selling and using gunpowder, fire-crackers or fire-works manufactured or prepared therefrom, or other combustible materials, and the exhibition of fire-works, and the discharge of fire-arms, and the lights in barns, stables and other buildings, and to restrain the making of bonfires in streets and yards; Gunpowder &c.

Eighth. To prevent the encumbering of streets, sidewalks, cross-walks, lanes, alleys, bridges, acqueducts, wharves or slips, in any manner whatever; Clearing streets, &c.

Ninth. To prevent and punish horse-racing and immoderate riding or driving in any street, and to authorize the stopping and detaining any person who shall be guilty of immoderate driving or riding in any street; Horse Racing, &c.

Tenth. To determine and designate the routes and grades of any railroad to be laid in said city, and to restrain and regulate the use of locomotives, engines and cars upon the railroads within the city. Railroads.

TITLE III. COMMON COUNCIL:—WHO SHALL CONSTITUTE; POWERS, &C., &C.

Bathing, &c. *Eleventh.* To prohibit or regulate bathing in any public water, and to provide for cleansing Saginaw River of drift-wood and other obstructions;

Vagrants, &c. *Twelfth.* To restrain and punish drunkards, vagrants, mendicants, street beggars, and persons soliciting alms or subscriptions for any purpose whatever;

Impounding animals. *Thirteenth.* To establish and regulate one or more pounds, and to restrain and regulate the running at large of horses, cattle, swine and other animals, geese and poultry, and to authorize the impounding and sale of the same for the penalty incurred, and the costs of keeping and impounding;

Dogs. *Fourteenth.* To regulate and prevent the running at large of dogs, to impose taxes on the owners of dogs, and to prevent dog fights in the streets;

Putrid Meats, Hides, &c. *Fifteenth.* To prohibit any person from bringing and depositing within the limits of said city, any dead carcass or other unwholesome or offensive substances; and to require the removal or destruction thereof, if any person shall have on his premises such substances, or any putrid meats, fish, hides or skins of any kind, and on his default, to authorize the removal or destruction thereof by some officer of the city;

Clearing of Sidewalks. *Sixteenth.* To compel all persons to keep side-walks in front of premises owned or occupied by them, clear from snow, dirt wood or obstructions;

Ringing of Bells. *Seventeenth.* To regulate the ringing of bells, and the crying of goods and other commodities for sale at auction or otherwise; and to prevent disturbing noises in the streets;

Watchmen. *Eighteenth.* To prescribe the powers and duties of Watchmen and the fines and penalties for their delinquencies;

Burial of dead. *Nineteenth.* To regulate the burial of the dead, and compel the keeping and return of bills of mortality;

Regulate Markets. *Twentieth.* To establish, order and regulate the markets, and to prohibit forestalling the same, to regulate the vending of wood, meats, vegetables, fruits, fish and provisions of all kinds, and prescribe the time and place for selling the same, and the fees to be paid by butchers for license: Proviso. *Provided*, That nothing herein contained shall authorize the Common Council to restrict in any way the sale of fresh and wholesome meats by the quarter, within the limits of the city, at any time later than nine o'clock in the morning of each day; Reservoirs, &c.

Twenty-first. To establish, regulate and preserve public reservoirs, wells and pumps; and to prevent the waste of water; Concerning Sextons, Porters and others.

Twenty-second. To adopt rules for the regulation of sextons and undertakers in burying the dead; also for carmen and their carts, hackney carriages and their drivers, omnibuses and their drivers, scavengers, porters and chimney sweeps, and their fees and compensation, and the fees to be paid by them into the City Treasury for licenses;

Twenty-third. To prevent runners, stage drivers and others, from soliciting passengers or others to travel or ride in any stage, omnibus, boat, or upon any railroad, or to go to any hotel or otherwheres; Runners.

Twenty-fourth. Concerning the lighting of the streets and alleys. and the protection and safety of public lamps; Lighting of Streets.

Twenty-fifth. To regulate and restrain hawking and peddling in the streets, and to regulate pawn-brokers; Peddling.

Twenty-sixth. To prescribe the duties of all officers appointed by the Common Council, and their compensation, and the penalty or penalties for failing to perform such duties, and to prescribe the bonds and sureties to be given by the officers of the city for the discharge of their duties, and the time for executing the same, in cases not otherwise provided for by law; Duties, Penalties and Bonds.

Twenty-seventh. To preserve the salubrity of the Waters of Saginaw River, or other streams within the limits of the said city; to fill up all low grounds or lots covered or partially covered with water, or to drain the same, as they may deem expedient; Saginaw River. Abate Nuisance.

Twenty-eighth. To prescribe and designate the stands for carriages of all kinds which carry persons for hire, and for carts and carters, and to prescribe the rates of fare and charges, and the stand or stands for wood, hay and produce exposed for sale in said city; Stands for Carriages, &c.

Twenty-ninth. To prescribe the line upon which docks shall be built in Saginaw River, and beyond which they shall not extend, and to enforce the same by a fine not exceeding five hundred dollars, and to regulate such docks, and to compel the owners or occupants thereof to keep the same in repair; Docks and Dock Lines. Penalty.

Harbor Masters. *Thirtieth.* To appoint so many harbor masters as they may deem necessary, and to prescribe their powers, duties and compensation.

Weights and Measures. *Thirty first.* To prescribe the duties of sealers of weights and measures, and the penalty for using false weights and measures, and all the laws of this State in relation to the sealing of weights and measures shall apply to said city, except as herein otherwise provided. [*Act of* 1859.]

Streets and Alleys. (§ 46.) SEC. 11. The Common Council may ascertain, establish and settle the boundaries of all streets and alleys in the said city, and prevent and remove all encroachments thereon, and exercise all other powers conferred on them by this Act, in relation to Taxes, Fires &c. highways, the prevention of fires, the levying of taxes, the supplying of the city with water, and all other subjects of municipal regulation, not herein expressly provided. [*Act of* 1859.]

Penalties Provided by Ordinance. (§ 47.) SEC. 12. Where, by the provisions of this Act, the Common Council have authority to pass ordinances on any subject, they may prescribe a penalty not exceeding one hundred dollars, (unless the imposition of a greater penalty be herein otherwise provided,) for a violation thereof, and may provide that the offender, on failing to pay the penalty imposed, shall be imprisoned in the county jail of Saginaw County, or in the city prison, for any term not exceeding ninety days, which penalties may be sued for and recovered, with costs, in the name of the City of East Saginaw. [*Act of* 1859.]

When Ordinances to take effect. (§ 48.) SEC. 13. No Ordinance of the Common Council imposing a penalty shall take effect until after the expiration of at least three days after the first publication thereof in a newspaper published in said city. [*Act of* 1859.]

Record to be used as evidence. (§ 49.) SEC. 14. A record or entry made by the Clerk of the said city, or a copy of such record or entry duly certified by him shall be prima facie evidence of the time of such first publication and all laws, regulations and ordinances of the Common Council may be read in evidence in all courts of justice, and in all proceedings before any officer, body or board in which it shall be necessary to refer thereto; either,

First. From a copy certified by the Clerk of the city, with the seal of the city of East Saginaw affixed; or,

Second. From the volume of ordinances printed by authority of the Common Council. [*Act of* 1859.]

(§ 50.) SEC. 15. Whenever the Common Council are required by law to make publication of any notices, ordinances, or resolutions or proceedings, in one or more newspapers of said city, it shall be deemed sufficient to publish the same in any daily or weekly newspaper published in said city. [*Act of* 1859.] Publication of Notices, &c.

(§ 51.) SEC. 16. The Common Council shall have power to purchase and to hold a suitable lot or lots of land, within or without the corporation limits, for the purpose of a City Cemetery or Cemeteries; and they shall make such rules and regulations regarding the same as they may deem necessary; and may cause the same to be surveyed into suitable lots, and may dispose of the same to purchasers, and thereupon cause to be executed to such purchaser a good and sufficient deed, in the corporate name of the said city, which deed shall be signed by the Mayor and Clerk, and countersigned by the Comptroller. [*Act of* 185.9] City Cemetery.

(§ 52.) SEC. 17. The Commissioners of the City Cemetery and the Comptroller, shall constitute a board of Superintendants of the City Cemetery, and the Comptroller shall be the Treasurer of said board. [*Act of* 1859.] Cemetery Commissioners.

(§ 53.) SEC. 18. The Common Council shall have power to purchase a Potter's Field, within or without the city limits, for the burial of the city poor, and may make such rules and regulations concerning the same as they may deem necessary. [*Act of* 1859.] Potter's Field.

(§ 54.) SEC. 19. The Common Council shall have power whenever, in their opinion, the necessities of the city require, to construct a City Alms House, City Hall and City Market or Markets, and to appoint the Keepers, Clerks, and necessary officers thereof, and may locate such City Alms House, City Hall and City Market or Markets, within or without the city limits, and may make such regulations concerning the same as the Common Council may think proper. [*Act of* 1859.] Almshouse, Market, City Hall, &c.

(§ 55.) SEC. 20. The Common Council shall have and exercise in and over said city, the same powers in relation to the regulation of Taverns, Groceries, Common Victualers, Saloon Keepers and others, as are now or may hereafter be conferred by the general laws of this State upon Township Boards, or upon the corpo- Innkeepers, Saloons &c.

rate authorities of Cities and Villages in relation to Tavern Keepers and Common Victualers, and subject to the same conditions and limitations; and the general laws of this State now in force, or which may hereafter be enacted, in relation to the regulation of Taverns, Groceries and Common Victualers, shall be deemed applicable to the city, unless otherwise limited. No person shall engage in or exercise the business or occupation of Tavern Keeper, Inn Holder, Common Victualer, or Saloon Keeper within the limits of said city, until he is first licensed as such by the Common Council; and any person who shall assume to exercise such business or occupation, without having first obtained such license, shall forfeit and pay, for every day he shall so exercise such occupation or business, the sum of two dollars, to be recovered by action of debt, in the name of the City of East Saginaw, before any justice of the peace of said city, together with the costs of prosecution. The Common Council shall have power to grant licenses to authorize persons to exercise the business of Tavern Keeper, Inn Holder, Common Victualer, or Saloon Keeper, within the said city, and may impose such fees to be paid into the City Treasury on the granting of such license, as they may see fit. [*Act of* 1859.]

Must first obtain a License.

Penalty.

Council may License, &c.

(§ 56. SEC. 21. On the last Tuesday before the last Monday in the month of March of each year, the Common Council shall audit and settle the accounts of all other officer and persons having claims against the city, or accounts with it; and shall make out a statement in detail of the receipts and expenditures of the corporation during the preceeding year, in which statement shall be clearly and distinctly specified the several items of expenditure made by the Common Council, the objects and purposes for which the same were made, and the amount of money expended under each, the amount of taxes raised for the general contingent expenses, the amount raised for lightning and watching the city, the amount of highway taxes and assessments, the amount of assessments for opening, paving, planking, repairing and altering streets, and building and repairing bridges, the amount borrowed on the credit of the city, and the terms on which the same was obtained, and such other information as shall be necessary to a full understanding of the financial concerns of the city. [*Act of* 1867.]

Common Council's Annual Report.

Contents of.

(§ 57.) SEC. 22. The said statement shall be signed by the Mayor and Clerk, and filed with the papers of the city; and the same shall be published by the Clerk, at the expense of the city, in some newspaper thereof, to be designated by the Common Council, previous to the first Monday of April thereafter. [*Act of* 1867.] Signed, filed and published.

(§ 58.) SEC. 23. The Common Council of the City of East Saginaw, or the major part of them, shall have the sole and exclusive power from time to time, to license, continue and regulate so many Ferries from within said City of East Saginaw to the opposite shore of Saginaw River, for the carriage and transportation of people, goods and chattels across the said river, in such manner as shall appear to them most conducive to the public good: *Provided*, That nothing contained in this section shall be so construed as to deprive any person whatever of the possession of the property or soil on the shore of said river, nor of any right of ferriage under any existing license. [*Act of* 1859.] Ferries.

(§ 59.) SEC. 24. The members of the Common Council shall be allowed, as compensation for their services, one dollar for actual attendance at each regular session of the Council, to be certified by the Clerk to the Controller, quarterly, and paid out of the general fund. [*Act of* 1869.] Compensation of members.

(§ 60.) SEC. 25. Any Alderman who shall be absent from the sessions of the Common Council, without leave, for six consecutive weeks, shall be deemed to have resigned, and the office shall be deemed vacant, and the Common Council shall order a new election to fill such vacancy, as in this act provided in case of vacancies. [*Act of* 1869.] Absence to vacate office

(§ 61.) SEC. 26. The Common Council shall have power to direct the deposit of all moneys, bonds, papers and evidences of value, in any bank, vault or safe, and receive interest on all balances and moneys so deposited, which interest received shall be credited to and from a part of the interest fund. [*Act of* 1869.] Deposit of moneys, &c.

(§ 62.) SEC. 27. The Common Council shall have power to expel or remove from office any of its own members, or any other officer holding office by election, except the Mayor and Recorder, for corrupt or wilful malfeasance or misfeasance in office, or for the wilful neglect of the duties of his office, by a vote of two-thirds of all the Aldermen elect; and in such case, the reasons for such ex- Expulsion and removal of Officers.

pulsion or removal, shall be entered upon the records of the Common Council, with the names and votes of the members voting on the question. But no officer holding office by election, shall be removed or expelled by said Common Council, unless first furnished with a copy of the charges against him in writing, and be allowed to be heard in his defence, with aid of counsel; and for the purposes hereof, the Common Council shall have power to issue subpœnas, to compel the attendance of witnesses, to examine witnesses upon oath to be administered by the presiding officer, and the production of papers, when necessary, and shall proceed within ten days after service of a copy of the charges, to hear and determine upon the case. If any such officer shall neglect to appear and answer to said charges, his default shall be deemed good cause for his removal from office. [*Act of* 1869.]

TITLE IV.

OFFICERS:—THEIR RIGHTS, POWERS AND DUTIES.

(§ 63.) SEC. 1. It shall be the duty of the Mayor to take care that the laws of the State, and the ordinances of the Common Council be faithfully executed; to exercise a constant supervision and control over the conduct of all subordinate officers, and to receive and examine into all complaints against them for neglect of duty; to recommend to the Common Council such measures as he shall deem expedient; to expedite such as shall be resolved by them, and, in general, to maintain the peace and good order, and advance the prosperity of the city. [*Act of* 1859.] Duties of the Mayor.

(§ 64.) SEC. 2. All official bonds of said city shall be deposited with the Clerk of the city for safe keeping, unless the Council otherwise order, in which case they shall be deposited as they Official bonds, when deposited.

may direct; and it shall be his duty to deliver the same to his successor in office. [*Act of* 1859.]

Duties of Aldermen

(§ 65.) SEC. 3. It shall be the duty of every Alderman in said city to attend the regular and special meetings of the Common Council; to act upon committees when thereunto appointed by the Mayor or Common Council; to order the arrest of all persons violating the laws of this State, or the ordinances, by-laws or police regulations; to report to the Mayor all subordinate officers who are guilty of any official misconduct or neglect of duty; to maintain peace and good order, and to perform all other duties required of them by this act. [*Act of* 1859.]

Special duties of the Mayor, Recorder and Aldermen.

(§ 66.) SEC. 4. The Mayor, Recorder and Aldermen, by virtue of their respective offices, shall be conservators of the public peace, and as such, shall each have and exercise all the power and authority of Justices of the Peace in criminal cases, and in enforcing the laws of the State, relating to the police thereof, but shall have no jurisdiction of civil cases, other than such as by this act shall be expressly conferred upon them, or either of them. [*Act of* 1859.]

Controller, when appointed and duties of.

(§ 67.) SEC. 5. There shall be appointed by the Common Council at their first meeting in the month of March, 1865, and at their third regular meeting in the month of April, every three years thereafter, or as soon thereafter as may be, one Controller, who shall hold his office for the term of three years. It shall be the duty of the Controller to keep the financial accounts of said corporation to countersign all bonds, orders upon the treasury, licenses, burial permits, cemetery deeds, and all evidences of debt and transfer of property which the Common Council or corporation are authorized to issue or make, pledging the faith of said city; to receive all accounts and demands against the said corporation, examine them in detail, audit or allow them, or such parts thereof as to the correctness of which he has no doubt, and which the claimant is willing to accept in full discharge thereof, file and number them as vouchers, with the date of their allowance, and the funds out of which payable, and when so audited, settled, filed, dated and numbered, to report the same to the Common Council, and when payment shall be duly authorized by the Common Council, to countersign and register the orders drawn therefor by the City Clerk, upon the City Treasurer. No claim so audited shall be binding against the city until approved by vote of the Common

Keep Accounts.

Countersign Bonds, &c.

Receive and Audit all Accounts against the city.

Record of Bonds.

Council. The Controller shall keep a record of bonds issued by said corporation, with the number, amount and dates, when issued, when payable, and all coupons attached thereto, and shall keep account, in proper books, of all such bonds and the bonded indebtedness, for the information of the Common Council. And the Controller shall also, in like manner, keep accounts of all funds taxes, assessments, receipts and expenditures, and on the last Tuesday before the last Monday, in the month of March, in each year, shall make out and present a full statement and balance-sheet of the financial accounts of the city, with such recommendations and explanations as may be proper to add thereto. The Controller shall advertise and receive proposals for all contracts for or on be half of the city, except as in this act otherwise provided and report his action thereon to the Common Council. He shall sign all contracts and agreements on behalf of the city, except as in this act otherwise provided, subject to the orders of the Common Council, and make all purchases of materials, tools, books, stationery, apparatus, and property for the city or its officers, not otherwise provided for herein, or ordered by the Common Council. He shall keep a record of all officers and employees of the city, and certify the pay-rolls and wages of all such officers and persons to the Common Council; he shall be charged with the leasing, repairs, insurance and general supervision of the property of the city, and for his information may require reports from all officers and persons having any city property in charge or possession, and report upon the same when required by the Council. It shall also be the duty of the Controller to examine all tax rolls and reports of city officers, and transfer abstracts of the same to his account book, and take and exercise a general supervision of the financial concerns of the corporation; to keep complete sets of books, exhibiting the condition of said corporation in its various departments and funds, its resources and liabilities, with proper classification thereof, of each fund or appropriation for any distinct object of expenditure or class of expenditures. Whenever any such fund or appropriation has been exhausted by warrants already drawn thereon, or by appropriations, liabilities, debts, or expenses actually incurred or contracted for, the Controller shall advise the Council thereof at its next meeting. The Controller shall also be a member of and Treasurer of the Board of Cemetery Commissioners,

Funds, Taxes, &c.

Annual Report.

Receive proposals and make contracts.

Make Purchases.

Pay Roll.

Officers to report to.

Tax Rolls.

Books.

Funds.

Cemetery Commis'r.

and keep all records and accounts of said board, except as otherwise herein provided. The Controller shall open an account with the Treasurer, in which he shall charge said Treasurer with the whole amount of taxes, special or general, levied in said city and placed in his hands for collection, all sums received for licenses, rents, and all other moneys which may be paid into the city treasury, and all bonds, coupons, notes, leases, mortgages, interest, and bills receivable by said city, of whatever nature. He shall charge, to the several Ward Collectors all taxes which may be placed in their hands for collection, and all other officers of the corporation, with all funds, moneys, and property placed or being in their possession, and shall require settlement with such officers at least once in each year, and as much oftener, not to exceed once in each month as the interests of the city and the safety of its property may require and he shall give said Treasurer, Collectors and all other officers credits for all moneys disbursed, upon showing of proper vouchers, and for all property consumed, expended and destroyed by ordinary wear and use, and not otherwise. The Controller shall make out and attach warrants to all tax rolls of said city, whether for State, County, City, General or Special Assessments, or Taxes, and such warrants shall be in the usual form of law, and shall have the same virtue, force and legal effect as warrants made by the Supervisors of townships, pursuant to the laws of the State. The Controller shall also perform such other duties as are or may be prescribed by this act, or by ordinances of the Common Council, not inconsistent herewith, and shall receive for his services such annual salary as the Common Council shall prescribe, and he shall give a bond with sureties in the sum of not less than five thousand dollars, for the faithful performance of the duties hereby imposed. And the Controller shall have a seat in the Common Council, and may speak upon all matters that come before the Council, and serve upon committees thereof, but shall have no vote. [*Act of* 1869.]

Account of Treasurer. Account of Ward Collectors. Settlements. Credits, how given. Warrants to Tax Rolls. Bond.

Assessor; Appointments and duties of.

(§ 68.) SEC. 6. The Common Council shall, at their third meeting in the month of April, in the year 1869, or as soon thereafter as may be, and every three years thereafter, appoint one Assessor for said city, who shall annually assess all the property in said city liable to taxation under the laws of this State, now or hereafter in force, for the purpose of levying the taxes lawfully imposed thereon, and who shall, for the purpose of making such assessment, have all the powers, and perform all the duties of Supervisors of townships in this State. The Assessor shall also prepare and make the returns required by law, relative to the registration of births and deaths of said city, and the list of persons to serve as jurors, and perform such other duties as this act imposes. The Assessor, the Controller, the City Attorney, and the Supervisors elected in the several Wards, shall be members of the Board of Supervisors of Saginaw County, and represent the interests of this corporation on said board; and the Assessor, City Attorney and the Controller as such Supervisors, shall be entitled to receive the same compensation as other Supervisors, for attendance upon said board. The Assessor shall have power to administer oaths and affirmations, whenever necessary to the proper discharge of the duties of the office, and any person who shall wilfully swear falsely to any return, valuation, record, property, or material fact regarding his property liable to be assessed under the laws of this State. shall be held and deemed guilty of the crime of perjury. The Assessor shall receive such compensation, for his services in making assessments and levying and extending taxes thereon, as the Common Council may determine, and shall be subject to removal for cause the same as other officers appointed by the Common Council. [*Act of* 1869.]

Births, Deaths, Jurors.

Supervisors

Power to Administer Oaths.

Compensation.

(§ 69.) SEC. 7. The Wards of said City shall each constitute a separate Assessment District; *Provided*, The assessment rolls made and used for City purposes, may, for convenience, be enclosed in one book or volume, which shall be bound and preserved in the office of the City Clerk, for future reference and use of said city, as hereinafter provided. The assessment rolls of the several Wards for State and County purposes, shall not be so bound, but shall be made separately by Wards, in the manner, and for the purposes hereinafter provided and specified. [*Act of* 1869.]

Assessment Rolls.

(§ 70.) SEC. 8. The Supervisors of the several Wards of said city shall be members of the Board of Supervisors of Saginaw County, and shall perform all the duties of Supervisors of Townships, except as herein especially provided, and except as to such duties as are herein especially devolved upon other officers of said city, and shall be entitled to the same compensation as Township Supervisors, and to such additional compensation as is hereinbefore provided. [*Act of* 1869.]

Supervisors

City Clerk, duties of.

(§ 71.) SEC. 9. The Clerk shall keep the corporate seal, and all the papers and files belonging to said city as a corporation, not properly by this act in the custody of some other officer thereof, and shall make a full and complete record of the Proceedings of the Common Council, whose meetings it shall be his duty to attend; and copies of all papers duly filed in his office, and transcripts from the records of the proceedings of the Common Council, certified to by him under the corporate seal, shall be evidence in all places, when produced, of the matters therein contained; he shall attest all licenses granted for any purpose whatever by the Mayor or Common Council, and shall enter in an appropriate book, the name of every person to whom a license shall be granted, and the number of such license, and the date thereof, and the time during which it is to be continued in force, and the sum paid for such license; no license for any purpose granted shall be valid until thus attested by the Clerk and countersigned by the Controller. He shall also act as Clerk of the Board of Health and the Board of Water Commissioners of said city, and when so required, of the Standing Committees of the Common Council, and perform such other duties as may be required by law of township clerks, so far as applicable under this act or the ordinances of the city. [*Act of* 1869.]

Licenses.

Ordinances, &c., to be published

(§ 72.) SEC. 10. The Clerk shall publish at least one week in one of the newspapers printed in the city, all ordinances of the Common Council, for the violation of which any penalty may be imposed, and all votes, ordinances and resolutions, directing the payment of money, shall be published at least once in like manner, within eight days after the passage of such vote, ordinance or resolution; he shall also perform such other duties as this act shall direct, or which may be directed by ordinance of the Common Council. [*Act of* 1859.]

Treasurer, duties of.

(§ 73.) SEC. 11. The Treasurer shall receive all moneys belonging to the city, except such as are required to be kept in the hands of the Controller, and shall receive all taxes of said city, levied by order or authority of the Common Council, except as herein otherwise provided. The Treasurer shall alsh collect all rents, interest, claims and dues to said city, arising from rentals, leases, sales of property, or claims of any other nature whatever, not herein otherwise provided for. He shall hold all bonds, notes, mortgages and other evidences of debt or value belonging to the said corporation. He shall deposit the moneys of the city under the direction of the Common Council, and shall keep an accurate account of the same, and all receipts and expenditures thereof, and with every fund and appropriation thereof, made by this act, or by the authority and direction of the Common Council. He shall pay no money out of the treasury, except in pursuance of or by authority of law, or in satisfaction of warrants drawn by order of the Common Council, signed by the City Clerk and countersigned by the Controller, or of coupons and bonds regularly and lawful issued by said corporation. He shall keep an accurate account of and report to the Controller once in each week, a detailed statement of all taxes collected and moneys received, as well as all moneys disbursed, and at the end of every quarter shall make a full settlement with the Controller and Finance Committee of the Common Council, producing the vouchers for all transactions, which vouchers shall be canceled by said Controller and Committee, and the result of such settlement reported to the Council. Bonds and coupons shall be paid out of the particular funds constituted or raised for the purpose for which the same are issued, and warrants shall be paid only out of moneys in the funds against which the same are drawn as written upon the face thereof. Whenever any warrant is presented for payment, if there is no money in the fund upon which such warrant is drawn, the Treasurer shall endorse the date of such presentation on the back of such warrant, which shall thereafter draw interest at the rate of seven per cent. per annum, for a period not exceeding six months, unless the same shall be again presented for payment and endorsed, and the Treasurer shall compute interest as above provided, and pay the same when said warrant is redeemed, and charge the amount so paid for interest to the interest fund. The Treasurer shall keep an office in some convenient place in said city, and the books and accounts in his charge belonging to the city shall be open to the inspection of any tax-payer of said city at reasonable hours, in any week day (except in case of sickness or leave of absence ganted by the Common Council,) and where all bonds, coupons and warrants shall be presented for payment; and the Treasurer shall not discriminate as to parties holding bonds, coupons or warrants, or other lawful

Settlements

Interest on Warrants.

Keep an office.

Where money to be paid out.

demands, and shall pay them only when so presented at his office. The Treasurer shall obey all orders and resolutions of the Common Council, and perform all duties devolved upon him by this act or by resolution or ordinance of said Common Council, not inconsistent with the provisions of this act, and shall turn over to his successor in office all money, books, papers, and property of every kind and description, due and belonging to said corporation, upon demand. The Common Council shall have power to prescribe the percentage added to all tax rolls, not herein provided for, and to direct to what fund it shall be credited, and may direct the Treasurer as to the deposit and safe keeping of all books and papers of his office, and require bonds with such sureties and in such amount as they deem proper for the faithful performance of his duties as Treasurer; and said Treasurer shall receive for all services he may render, such annual salary as the Common Council may direct. [*Act of* 1869.]

Percentage to be added to Tax Rolls Bonds, &c.

Bonds, etc.

City Attorney.

(§ 74.) SEC. 12. The City Attorney shall be an attorney and counselor at law of good standing, and qualified to practice in all the courts in the State. He shall, on application of the Common Council, or of any officer of the city, furnish advice relative to all matters of law, in the discharge of their duties, appear in behalf of the city in all suits, and perform such other legal duties as may be prescribed by ordinance. [*Act of* 1869.]

Marshal, Powers and duties of.

Serve Process of Recorder's court.

Attend the Sessions of the Council.

Chief of Police.

Fire Warden.

(§ 75.) SEC. 13. The Marshall shall possess and exercise the powers and duties as conservator of the peace which township constables possess and may exercise by virtue of the laws of the State; he shall attend the sittings of the recorder's court, and be vested with full power and authority to serve papers and execute all process issued by said recorder's court; he, or his assistant, shall attend the sessions of the Common Council, and obey all orders received from the Mayor and Council; he shall, by virtue of his office, be chief of the police force of the corporation, and as such, perform all the duties required by the ordinances of the Common Council; he shall be superintendent of the city, and charged with its peace, and the execution and enforcement of the by-laws and ordinances thereof; he shall be chief fire warden of the city, and attend all fires, and report to the Mayor, and, whenever necessary, to the Common Council, any drunkenness and disorderly conduct among firemen, and shall have summary power, and it shall be his duty, to arrest, or cause to be arrested, all members of the fire department, or other persons who shall be drunk or disorderly at fires; he shall report, in writing, to the Mayor. the origin, extent and cause of all fires, with such information as will tend to check incendiarism and preserve property; he shall be the fence viewer of the city, and for that purpose, is hereby vested with the same powers and duties, and entitled to the same compensation as is now or may be prescribed by the laws of the State for fence viewers in townships; he shall perform such other duties as may from time to time be imposed by the laws of the State, or by the resolutions, orders and ordinances of the Common Council, and shall receive, in addition to his annual salary, such fees for the performance of the duties of the office, as are allowed to sheriff's or constables in like cases, except where such fees are a charge against the city treasury. The Assistant Marshal shall have and exercise the same powers as the Marshal, except as fence viewer, and as limited by ordinances of the Common Council. [*Act of* 1869.]

Incendiarism.

Fence Viewer.

Fees.

Assistants.

(§ 76.) SEC. 14. The Recorder shall possess the same powers and peform and discharge the municipal duties of Mayor during the absence, inability, death, resignation or removal of the Mayor; he shall also have power to hold a recorder's court, with such jurisdiction and powers as are hereinafter prescribed, and he shall have the power, and may exercise the jurisdiction, in all cases arising within the limits of the said city, which is now or may hereafter be conferred upon the Circuit Court Commissioners of the State, under proceedings for the collection of demands against ships, boats and vessels, by chapter one hundred and twenty-two of the revised statutes of the State, aud the amendments thereof; also in cases of proceedings to recover the possession of land in certain cases, by chapter one hundred and twenty-three of said revised statutes and the amendments thereof; also in cases of habeas corpus and certiorari, to inquire into causes of detention by chapter one hundred and thirty-four of said revised statutes; and in the exercise of such jurisdictions, shall be entitled to demand and receive the same fees for the services so rendered, as are now or may hereafter be allowed to Circuit Court Commissioners for like services; the Recorder shall be entitled to a seat within the Common Council for the purpose of deliberation, and of acting on committees, but

Recorder, Powers and duties of.

shall have no vote therein except when performing the duties of Mayor, according to the provisions of this act. [*Act of* 1859.]

Justice of the Peace, Powers of.

(§ 77.) SEC. 15. The Justices of the Peace of said city shall file their oaths of office in the office of the clerk of the County of Saginaw, and shall have, in addition to the jurisdiction conferred by this act on them, the same jurisdiction, powers and duties conferred on Justices of the Peace in townships, and shall have concurrent jurisdiction with the recorder's court of said city, of all actions brought for the recovery of any fine, penalty or forfeiture imposed by this act or any ordinance of said city, where such fine, penalty or forfeiture shall not exceed one hundred dollars, and when there shall not be in addition to such fine, penalty or forfeiture, any imprisonment by such law or ordinance for the violation thereof exceeding thirty days. [*Act of* 1867.]

Duties and Fees.

(§ 78.) SEC. 16. It shall be the duty of the Justices of the Peace of said city, to keep their offices in said city, and attend to all complaints of a criminal nature which may properly come before them, and they shall receive for their services when engaged in cases for violation of the ordinances of said city, such fees as the Common Council shall by ordinance prescribe. [*Act of* 1859.]

To account for all moneys, &c.

(§ 79.) SEC. 17. All fines, penalties or forfeitures, recovered before any of the Justices, shall, when collected, be paid into the city treasury; and each of said Justices shall report on oath to the Common Council, at the first regular meeting thereof, in each month during the term for which he shall perform the duties of such Justice, the number and name of every person against whom judgment shall have been rendered for such fine, penalty or forfeiture, and all moneys by him received, for or on account thereof, which moneys so received, or which may be in his hands, collected on such fine, penalty or forfeiture, shall be paid into the said city treasury on the first Monday of each and every month during the time such justice shall exercise the duties of said office; and for any neglect in this particular, he may be suspended or removed, as hereinafter provided. [*Act of* 1859.]

Penalty.

May be suspended or removed.

(§ 80.) SEC. 18. Any Justice of the Peace of said city may be suspended or removed from his said office by the circuit court of the County of Saginaw, for neglect or refusal to pay over as required by law, any moneys by him collected for or on account of any fine, penalty or forfeiture; or the unfaithful or insufficient performance of his duties in relation to the internal police of the State, or for any official misconduct, on charges specifically preferred, by said Common Council of said city or any member or officer thereof, or by three electors of said city, founded on affidavit filed in said circuit court, specifically stating the charges complained of, a copy whereof shall be served upon him at least ten days before presenting such charges to said court, and opportunity shall be given him to be heard in his defense. [*Act of* 1859.]

(§ 81.) SEC. 19. In addition to the security now required by law to be given by Justices of the Peace, each of the Justices of the Peace shall, before entering upon the duties of his office, execute a bond to the City of East Saginaw, with one or more sufficient sureties, to be approved by the Mayor or Recorder of said city; which approval shall be endorsed on said bond, in the penalty of one thousand dollars, conditioned for the faithful performance of his duties as a Police Justice of said city, and to pay over the moneys so collected, and make his report as in this act required; which bond shall be filed in the office of the Treasurer of said city. [*Act of* 1859.] **Security.**

(§ 82.) SEC. 20. All dockets and office books, kept by the Justices of the Peace, shall at all times be subject to inspection and examination by the Common Council, or any member or officer thereof, and it shall be the duty of said Justices of the Peace to produce such dockets and books at all times, whenever and wherever the said Common Council shall require or direct; and if they shall neglect or refuse to produce such docket or office book as directed and required, the Recorder may, on a proper application to him for the purpose, make an order requiring the same to be produced, and enforce obedience thereto in the same manner in which other orders made by the recorder's court are enforced. [*Act of* 1859.] **Dockets and Books.**

(§ 83.) SEC. 21. It shall be the duty of each Justice of the Peace at the first regular meeting of the Common Council in each of the months of August, November, February and May, in every year, to account on oath, before the Common Council, for all such moneys, goods, wares and merchandise seized as stolen property, as shall then remain unclaimed in the offices of either of said **Unclaimed Property, how disposed of, and accounted for.**

Justices of the Peace, and immediately thereafter to give notice for four weeks, in one of the public newspapers printed in the said City of East Saginaw, to all persons interested or claiming such property: *Provided, always*, That if any goods, wares, merchandise, or chattels of a perishable nature, or which shall be expensive to keep, shall at any time remain unclaimed in the offices of either of said Justices, it shall be lawful for such Justice to sell the same at public auction, at such time and after such notice, as to him and the said Common Council shall seem proper. [*Act of* 1859.]

Ibid. (§ 84.) SEC. 22. It shall be the duty of each of the Justices of the Peace aforesaid, who may recover or obtain possession of any stolen property, on his receiving satisfactory proof of property, from the owner, to deliver such property to the owner thereof, on his paying all necessary and reasonable expenses, which may have been incurred in the recovering, preservation or sustenance of such property, and the expenses of advertising the same. [*Act of* 1859.]

Ibid. (§ 85.) SEC. 23. It shall be the duty of each of the Justices of the Peace aforesaid, to cause all property unclaimed after the expiration of the notice specified in the last preceeding section but one of this act, money excepted, to be sold at public auction to the highest bidder, unless the Prosecuting Attorney of the County of Saginaw shall direct that it shall remain unsold for a longer period, to be used as evidence in the administration of justice, and the proceeds thereof forthwith to pay to the Treasurer of the said City of East Saginaw, together with all money, if any, which shall remain in his hands after such notice as aforesaid, first deducting the charges of said notice of sale. [*Act of* 1859.]

Police Constables. (§ 86.) SEC. 24. The Police Constables of said city shall have and receive the same fees, and have the like powers and authority, in matters of a criminal nature, as is conferred by law upon constables in the several towns of this State, and shall, if required by the Common Council, give like security, and each City Constable shall possess the same powers and be under the same duties and obligations as constables of townships, and shall give like security. [*Act of* 1859.]

Ibid (§ 87.) SEC. 25. The City Constables and Police Constables shall obey the orders of the Mayor, Recorder and Aldermen, or of any person legally exercising the criminal jurisdiction of a Justice of the Peace in said city, in enforcing the laws of the State or the ordinances of said city, and in case of refusal or neglect so to do, he or they shall be subject to a penalty of not less than one, nor more than twenty-five dollars. [*Act of* 1859.]

Criminal expenses paid by county.

(§ 88.) SEC. 26. The expenses of examining and committing offenders against any law of this State, in the said city, and of their confinement, shall be audited, allowed and paid by the Supervisors of the County of Saginaw, in the same manner as if such expenses had been incurred in any town of said county. [*Act of* 1859].

Street Commissioner, duties of.

(§ 89) SEC. 27. The Common Council shall annually, at their third meeting in the month of April in each year, or as soon thereafter as may be, appoint one Street Commissioner of said city, who shall superintend the construction and repairs and cleaning of all pavements side-walks, cross-walks, culverts, bridges, drains and sewers, and direct the working, cleaning and improvement of highways, streets, lanes, alleys, parks and public places in said city, not otherwise provided for under the direction of the Common Council. He shall keep an accurate record of all moneys received and disbursed, and of all persons, together with the number of horses, carts and wagons employed by him in the several wards, and render, under oath, to the Controller, each week, a true account of the time of each, and the expenses thereof, and the fund or funds out of which the same are payable. The Street Commissioner shall perform such other duties as may be required by resolution or ordinances of the Common Council, not inconsistent with the nature of his duties or the provisions of this act: *Provided*, That nothing in this act contained shall be construed to prevent the Common Council from paving, macadamizing, graveling, or otherwise improving or cleaning the streets, alleys, lanes, parks or public places of said city by contract, in case the Common Council shall decide to let such work to the lowest responsible bidder. [*Act of* 1869.]

Cemetery Commis'rs.

(§ 90.) SEC 28. The Superintendents of the City Cemetery or Cemeteries shall have care of the City Cemetery or Cemeteries and all the grounds or other property belonging thereto, subject to the ordinances and directions of the Common Council, they shall make such improvements upon the property as they shall think expedient, but shall not expend in any one year more than three hundred dollars, without the consent of the Common Council previously obtained, and they shall receive no pecuniary compensation for their services; and said Superintendents shall report quarterly to the Common Council the amount expended by them in the improvement of said property. [*Act of* 1859.]

Moneys and Expenses. (§ 91.) SEC. 29. The Controller shall, as treasurer of the Board, receive all moneys for lots which shall be sold in said City cemetery or cemeteries, and also all penalties collected for violation of city ordinances in relation to such cemetery or cemeteries, and shall pay, upon resolution of the board, for improvements made upon the grounds of the said cemetery or cemeteries, and also the incidental expenses of the board, when the accounts for said incidental expenses shall have been audited and allowed by the Superintendents. [*Act of* 1859.]

Ibid. (§ 92.) SEC. 30. The Controller shall pay over to the City Treasurer all moneys which shall come into his hands as treasurer the board of Superintendents of the city cemetery, which are of not by this act appropriated. [*Act of* 1859.]

Annual Report. (§ 93.) SEC. 31. It shall be the duty of said board of Superintendents to publish an annual report in relation to matters committed to their charge, in one of the newspapers printed in said city, between the first and fifteenth days of March in each year. [*Act of* 1867.]

School Inspectors. (§ 94.) SEC. 32. The School Inspectors of said city shall perform such duties as are required by the laws of the State, and the "Act to incorporate the Board of Education of the City of East Saginaw," approved February 15th, 1859, and the acts amendatory thereto: **Provided*, The said Inspectors shall be required to make and file with the Common Council on or before the third Monday in March, in each year, a detailed report of all receipts and expenditures of said board up to and including the last day of February, in each year, and such statement shall be published with and form a part of the annual statement of said city. [*Act of* 1869.]

Duties of Surveyor, Physician, &c. (§ 95.) SEC. 33 The City Surveyor, Health Physician, Fire Wardens, Common Criers, Pound Masters, Inspectors of fire wood and Weigh Masters, shall perform such duties, and if required,

* This Proviso repealed by act of 1869.

shall file such securities as the Common Council shall by ordinance direct.

(§ 96.) SEC. 34. The Common Council shall annually, at their first regular meeting in the month of May, or as soon thereafter as may be, determine or fix the salary or compensation to be paid to the several officers of said city, and they may also, from time to time, establish fees and compensation for all officers appointed by them, whose fees or salary are not prescribed by law, and whose compensation for services is required to be paid out of the city treasury. [*Act of* 1869.]

Salary of officers, when and how to be fixed.

(§ 97.) SEC. 35. The Collector of each Ward shall collect all State and County taxes assessed and imposed upon the real and personal property of the Ward, and such city, highway, sewer and school taxes, and all such special taxes as may be, from time to time, levied by the Common Council for the improvement of streets, the construction of sidewalks, or any other purposes authorized by this act or the laws of this State, as may be placed in his hands for collection by the Controller or other proper officer of said city, and the warrant of the Controller of said city shall confer full power and authority upon said Collector to collect, by levy and sale, all taxes set forth upon any copy or transcript of any general or special roll and so placed in his hands, the same as warrants made by supervisors of townships, under the laws of this State. All such Collectors shall give receipts for all taxes collected by them, and mark the same paid upon the proper rolls, and shall pay over all moneys in their hands, belonging to the city, to the city Treasurer, on Monday, of each week, and deposit with the Controller a detailed statement of all collections and a receipt from the Treasurer for the same, and shall make due returns of all rolls, and the uncollected taxes thereon, as required by the warrant of the Controller and the provision of this act and the laws of the State: *Provided*, The returns of all State and County taxes, and the uncollected taxes upon the city tax rolls shall be made direct to the County Treasurer of Saginaw County, as required by law; and a copy of the returns of all such city taxes, with a receipt from the City Treasurer for all moneys due on the same shall also be filed with the Controller by the Collector, within ten days after the time specified in the warrant for the return

Collectors of Taxes.

Power of Warrant.

Receipts.

Pay over moneys.

Return of Warrant.

Copy to be filed with Controller.

Bonds. of said roll. Each of said Collectors shall give bonds to the city of East Saginaw, in such amount and with such sureties, as the Common Council may require, in a sum not exceeding twice the amount of the taxes placed in their hands for collection; and the Controller or Common Council may require additional bonds, from time to time, as the public interests may require. Fees. For the collection of all city taxes and special assessments, said Collectors shall be entitled to receive the sum of four per cent, upon all moneys actually collected and paid into the city treasury by them, which amount shall be paid by the city Treasurer to said Collector upon the certificate of the Controller that the Collector has fully complied with the requirements of his warrant and the provisions of this act. How Bonds shall be discharged. The bonds required by the city from Ward Collectors shall be deposited with the Controller; and whenever final settlement is made with such Collector, the Controller shall endorse the same upon said bond, which endorsement shall operate as a full discharge of said Collector and his sureties, unless it shall afterwards appear that the returns filed by said Collector, in whole or in part, were false, in which case such bond shall continue in force; and such Collector and his sureties shall be liable therefor for all damages occasioned by such false returns. False Returns.

Vacancy provided for. In case any person elected as Ward Collector shall refnse to serve, or shall die, resign or remove out of said city before he shall have entered upon, or completed the duties of his office, or be disabled, from any cause, from completing the same, the Common Council shall forthwith appoint a Collector for the remainder of the year, who shall give like security, and be subject to like duties and penalties, and have the same powers and compensation as if regularly elected to said office of Collector, and the City Clerk shall immediately give notice of such appointment to the County Treasurer of Saginaw County; Clerk to give notice. but such appointment shall not operate to discharge or exonorate the former Collector, or his sureties, from any liability incurred by him, while acting as Collector: Proviso. *Provided,* Nothing in this act contained shall be construed to prevent the giving of bonds to the County Treasurer, which bond shall be approved, as required by law.

(§ 98.) SEC. 36. The Director of the Poor shall perform such duties as are imposed by law upon such officers in townships, and such other duties as may be imposed by ordinance. Director of Poor. All expenditures of money, and all accounts made by him, shall be duly certified under oath, to the Controller, as often, and in such manner, as the Common Council may require.[a] [*Act of* 1869.]

(§ 99.) SEC. 37. The Mayor, Recorder and Aldermen of said city, the City Clerk, Clerk of the Recorder's Court and Controller, are authorized generally to administer oaths and take affidavits, but neither of such officers shall receive any fees therefor, except the clerks. The Controller shall have power to take acknowledgments of deeds under the laws of this State, and to certify copies of all papers in his office, and receive the legal fees therefor. [*Act of* 1869.] Administer Oaths, &c.

(§ 100.) SEC. 38. Whenever any officer shall resign or be removed from office, or the term for which he shall have been elected or appointed shall expire, he shall on demand, deliver over to his successor in office, all the books, papers, moneys and effects of said corporation in his possession or custody as such officer, and in any way appertaining to his office; and every person violating this provision shall be deemed guilty of a misdemeanor, and may be proceeded against in the same manner as public officers generally for the like offense under the general laws of this State, now or hereafter in force or applicable thereto; and every officer appointed or elected under this act, shall be deemed an officer within the meaning and provisions of such general laws of this State. [*Act of* 1869.] Officers to deliver to their successors all books, &c. Penalty.

(§ 101.) SEC. 39. In addition to the rights, powers, duties and liabilities of officers prescribed in this act, all officers, whether elected or appointed, shall have such other rights, duties, powers or liabities, subject to and consistent with the provisions of this act, as the Common Council may deem expedient, and shall prescribe by resolution, by-laws or ordinance. [*Act of* 1869.] Additional Rights and Duties.

(§ 102.) SEC. 40. If any officer of the corporation shall, directly or indirectly, appropriate or convert any of the moneys, securities, evidences of value, or any property whatsoever belonging to the corporation, to his own use, or shall knowingly appropriate or convert the same to any other purpose than that for which such moneys, securities or evidences of value, or property may have been appropriated, raised or received, he shall be deemed guilty of willful and corrupt malfeasance in office, and may be prosecuted, tried Malfeasance in office.

[a] vide Sec. 1; Title 8.

Penalty. and convicted therefor, and on conviction, may be punished by fine not exceeding one thousand dollars, or imprisonment in the State prison or the jail of Saginaw County, not to exceed one year, or by both such fine and imprisonment, in the discretion of the court. [*Act of* 1869.]

TITLE V.

TAXES, FUNDS, REVENUES AND EXPENDITURES.

(§ 103.) SEC. 1. The resources and moneys of the corporation shall be controlled by the Common Council, as herein provided; and the said Common Council is hereby vested with the power to order assessments, direct the levying of taxes thereon, and provide for the collection of the same, under the provisions and restrictions in this act contained; and all assessments, taxes and revenues of said corporation shall be paid into and form a part of one of the following named funds, viz: *Power to levy and collect Taxes and control resources of the city vested in the Council.*

1st. General Fund, which shall be appropriated to defray the expenses of the City of East Saginaw, for the payment of which, out of some other fund, no provision is herein or otherwise made. *General Fund.*

2d. Highway Fund, to defray the expenses of repairing paved, *Highway Fund.*

graded, planked and improved streets, and for the construction and repair of crosswalks, bridges, drains, culverts, the cleaning of streets, sidewalks, drains, parks and public places, and such other general highway purposes as the Common Council may direct.

Fire Dep't Fund. 3d. Fire Department Fund, which shall be appropriated to defray the expense of purchasing lots, erecting engine houses thereon, purchasing engines and other fire apparatus, paying the regularly appointed firemen of the city, and all other expenses incident and necessary to the maintenance of the fire department of said city.

Sinking Fund. 4th. Sinking Fund, to redeem the bonds and pay the funded debt of the city.

Interest Fund. 5th. Interest Fund, to pay the interest on the funded debt of the city.

Sewer Fund 6th. Sewer Fund, to defray the expenses of building, repairing and maintaining the public sewers of the city, and for paying the interest and principal of bonds, issued by the corporation for sewerage purposes.

Poor Fund. 7th. Poor Fund, to defray the expenses of providing for and taking care of the poor of the city.

Sidewalk Funds. 8th. Sidewalk Fund, to defray the expenses of constructing sidewalks in said city, as provided in title six of this act.

Street Imp't Fund. 9th. Street Improvement Funds, to be assessed, levied and collected as hereinafter provided in title six of this act.

Other Funds. 10th. Such other Funds as are herein provided for, or as the Common Council may constitute for special purposes, not inconsistent with the provisions of this act, not to be taken from any of the funds above provided for, excepting the general fund. [*Act of* 1869.]

Tax may be levied. General Expenses. (§ 104.) SEC. 2. For the purpose of defraying the ordinary expenses and liabilities incurred by said city, and paying the same the Common Council may raise annually, by tax levied upon the real and personal property within said city, for the general fund, such sum as they may deem necessary, not exceeding one and one-half per cent. on the valuation of such real and personal estate within the limits of said city, according to the valuation thereof, taken from the assessment roll of the year preceding the levying of such tax; and the Common Council may, in addition thereto, Highway Purposes. levy such sum, not exceeding three-fourths of one per cent. of the valuation of the preceding year, as they may deem necessary for highway purposes, to be paid into the highway fund; and the Common Council may also, in addition to the above, levy such sum, not exceeding three mills on the dollar of the valuation of the preceding year, as they may deem necessary for defraying the expenses and making improvements in the fire department, to be credited to the fire department fund, and which shall be raised, assessed and collected on the same roll and in the same manner as the other city taxes. If the said Common Council shall deem it expedient for the purposes of the city, to levy a larger tax than is allowed by this section, they may, by giving ten days notice, by publishing the same in a newspaper published in said city, and posting a notice thereof in three public places in each ward in said city, call a meeting of the inhabitants of said city, at some place therein, who may then and there vote to levy, assess and collect a further money tax upon all the real and personal property in said city, in such sum as the meeting shall direct; and such tax shall be levied, assessed and collected in the same manner as is provided for the levying or collection of the other taxes mentioned in this act: *Provided*, That no person shall vote at such meeting who is not an elector in said city. The Mayor of said city shall preside or in his absence, the then acting Mayor shall preside at such meeting; and in the absence of both the Mayor and Recorder, the electors present may select one of their number to preside at such meeting. [*Act of* 1869.]

Expenses of Fire Dep't

Additional Tax may be voted by the citizens.

Proviso.

(§ 105.) SEC. 3. The moneys assessed by the Common Council under the authority of this act, for licenses and permits, and all fines imposed for the violation of the ordinances of the city, except as herein otherwise provided, shall be paid into and constitute the Poor Fund of said city. And in case of any deficiency in said fund, the Common Council shall have power, and it shall be their duty to appropriate from the general fund and transfer to the poor fund, such sum or sums as may be necessary for the proper care and keeping of the poor of said city.[a] [*Act of* 1869.]

Licences, &c., to go to Poor Fund.

Deficiency provided for

(§ 106.) SEC. 4. It shall be the duty of the Common Council, on or before the first day of June in each year, to determine by resolution the amount necessary to be raised by tax for city purposes within said city for such year; and it shall be the duty of

Council to determine amount to be raised.

Duty of Clerk.

[a] Vide Title 8, Sec. 6.

the City Clerk to certify the amount so to be raised to the Assessor, and it is hereby made the duty of the Assessor of said city to levy the sum so certified, and such other taxes as may be required by law, upon the taxable property of said city, in the same manner as specified in section seven of this title. [*Act of* 1869.]

Duty of the Assessor.

When Roll to be completed.

(§ 107.) SEC. 5. The Assessor of said city shall complete his annual assessment of all the taxable property in said city, on or before the fourth Monday in May, and upon the completion thereos, shall file a notice thereof with the City Clerk, who shall report the same to the Common Council at their next meeting. [*Act of* 1869.]

Board of Review.

Duties and Powers of Board.

Time and Place of meeting.

Sessions of Board.

May administer Oaths.

(§ 108.) SEC. 6. The Assessor, City Attorney and Supervisors of said city shall constitue a Board of Review, five of whom shall constitute a quorum. They shall elect one of their number Chairman, and the Assessor shall act as Secretary of the Board. They shall have power, and it shall be their duty to examine said assessment and correct any errors found therein, and on cause shown, to reduce, equalize, or increase the valuation of any property found on said rolls, and to add thereto any taxable property in said city that may have been omitted, and to value the same. They shall meet at such time and place as shall be appointed by the Common Council, of which time and place notice shall be given by the Clerk of said Council at least ten days prior to the time of meeting, by publishing a notice thereof in some newspaper published in said city, and also by posting the same in three public places in each ward of said city, and shall continue in session at least three days successively, and as much longer as may be necessary, at least six hours in each day, during said three days; and any person desiring so to do, may examine his or her assessment on said rolls, and may show cause, if any, why the valuation thereof should be changed, and the said board shall decide the same, and their decision shall be final. The concurrence of a majority of a quorum of said board, shall be sufficient to decide any question of altering or correcting any assessment complained of; and the members of the board shall have the power to administer oaths and examine witnesses, as provided for Supervisors of Townships, by the general laws of this State. The said board shall keep a record of their proceedings, and all changes made by them in said rolls, and their record shall be signed by a majority of said board, and deposited with the City Clerk. [*Act of* 1869.] Record

(§ 109.) SEC. 7. The said Assessor shall deliver the assessment roll to said board of review at their first meeting, and after the same shall be confirmed by resolution of said board, to be entered on their records, the said assessor shall again take such roll into his possession, and cause the amount of all taxes, in dollars and cents, authorized to be assessed and collected in each year, to be ratably assessed to each person named on lots described upon, and according to the aggregate valuation such person or lots shall have been assessed in said assessment roll, or book prepared as herein provided for that purpose, to be known as the annual tax roll of said city, in separate columns, showing the amount of highway, school, sewer and other city taxes assessed according to this act, to each person or lots in each year, and when said roll has been completed, and footed and balanced, which shall be on or before the first Monday in July. the said Assessor shall deliver said assessment roll to the controller, who shall make entry of the same, and of the totals of all taxes assessed thereon, on the books of his office, and the said Controller shall within one week thereafter, deposit said roll with the City Treasurer, with an order for its collection, as hereinafter provided, and the Treasurer shall give a receipt therefor, and be charged therewith, and shall thereupon and thereafter receive the taxes assessed thereon as hereinafter directed. And for all taxes and assessments on said roll not collected by said Treasurer, such proceedings shall be had for their collection and return as is in this act provided. [*Act of* 1869.] Assessor to spread taxes on Rolls. When to be completed and delivered to Controller. Duties of Controller and Treasurer.

(§ 110.) SEC. 8. Upon the receipt of the tax-rolls by the Treasurer, as hereinbefore provided, the taxes therein stated shall become due and payable, and the Treasurer shall forthwith, upon receiving said tax-roll, give public notice by publication in one or more papers in said city, and by posting the same in at least six public places in each ward of said city, which notice shall be a sufficient demand for the payment of all taxes upon said rolls. Such notice shall set forth that the said rolls have been deposited with him for collection, and that payment of the taxes therein specified may be made to him at any time before the last Saturday When taxes to become due and payable. Treasurer to give notice. What notice shall contain.

in December thereafter; that no addition will be made to taxes paid before the first day of August next thereafter, but that an addition of one per cent. of every unpaid tax will be made thereto, on that day, and like addition of one per cent. every thirtieth day thereafter, until such addition shall amount to six per cent. And said Treasurer shall thereupon receive all taxes paid to him according to the terms of said notice, except as to such taxes as are assessed upon property other than real estate hereinafter mentioned and specified, and provided for, adding thereto, on the first day of August, one per cent. of every such tax or assessment then unpaid, and an additional one per cent. thereto every thirtieth day thereafter, until the last Saturday in December. Upon the receipt of any tax, the Treasurer shall mark the same paid upon the proper tax roll, adding after the word "paid," the day and month when so paid, and shall in all cases give a receipt for the tax or taxes received, to the party paying the same. On the Monday succeeding the last Saturday in December, the Treasurer shall return the said tax-roll to the Controller, who shall give him a receipt for the same, and credit him with the amount of taxes on said roll, unpaid; and the Controller shall thereupon make out, in duplicate a copy of all assessments, and of the unpaid taxes thereon in each ward, which shall be a substantial transcript of such portion of the original tax rolls as relate to the unpaid taxes, adding six per cent. to the amount of each tax or assessment so unpaid, and exhibiting the original tax, and in the last column, the tax as augmented by the per cent. hereinbefore provided; one copy of said duplicate transcript shall be for record in the Controller's office and the other for the use of the proper Ward Collector to collect the same; and the Controller shall attach a warant thereto and deliver the same to the proper Ward Collector, who shall receipt for and be charged with the same, and said warrant shall command said Collector to collect the amounts due upon said rolls or transcripts of the annual tax roll, in the same manner as State and County taxes are collected, and to make return of the same to the County Treasurer of Saginaw County, as required by the general laws of this State, now, or hereafter in force for the collection and return of taxes by Township Treasurers; and said Collector shall make a duplicate return of all uncollected city taxes to the Controller, as hereinbefore provided; but the Common

Duties of the Treasurer.

Duties of Controller.

Deliver Roll and Warrant to Collector

Duty of Collector.

Tax on Personal Property.

Council may, by resolution, direct the Controller, at any time after the first day of August in each year, to make out transcripts or copies of any taxes remaining due and unpaid on said assessment roll, for each ward, and which are assessed wholly or partly against any property or value other than real estate, together with such percentage as shall be fixed by the Common Council, as compensation for the collection of such taxes or assessments, and to be stated in such rolls, and warrants shall be issued and annexed to each tax or assessment, signed by the Controller, and under the corporate seal of the corporation, directed to the proper Ward Collector, and made returnable upon such day as shall be designated by the Common Council, commanding him to collect from the persons named in the said transcript rolls the assessment and taxes therein specified and set forth as due from such persons, and for such purpose, if necessary, to levy upon and sell the personal property of such person, occupant or lessee refusing or neglecting to pay the same, wherever the same may be found within the limits of said city, and to pay over and account for the taxes or assessments thus collected, as herein provided. The Controller shall credit the Treasurer with the amounts of the taxes or assessments upon which warrants may be issued by order of the Common Council, and charge the same to the Collector to whom the same is delivered, and take a receipt therefor. Warrants for the collection of taxes, in the hands of the Collectors, may be renewed and extended by the Common Council from time to time but the time of the payment of any general tax shall not be extended beyond the time for the return of the State and County taxes, as fixed by law. [*Act of* 1869.]

Credits.

Warrants may be extended and renewed.

(§ 111.) SEC. 9. By virtue of the warrants by this act authorized to be issued by the Controller, the several Collectors to whom they may be respectively directed, shall have power to levy upon the personal property of persons from whom taxes may be due, wherever the same may be found within the limits of said city, and shall sell the same, in the same manner and with the same duties and powers of proceedings as now or hereafter may be provided by the laws of this State, for the collection of State and County taxes by Township Treasurers or Collectors. [*Act of* 1869.]

Powers of Warrant.

TITLE V. TAXES, FUNDS, REVENUES AND EXPENDITURES.

Treasurer to pay over School moneys weekly.

(§ 112.) SEC. 10. The City Treasurer shall pay over to the Board of Education, all moneys belonging to the school fund at least once in each week, taking duplicate receipts therefor, one of which shall be filed with the Controller; he shall keep a separate account of all moneys received for percentage in excess of the tax stated upon the several tax rolls, which amounts shall be exhibited in his weekly statement to the Controller, and which shall be credited to the interest fund. [*Act of* 1869.]

Per centage.

When Tax to become a lien.

(§ 113.) SEC. 11. The taxes assessed for city purposes upon any real estate of any resident or non-resident, and all legal charges made thereon, shall be a tax against the person owning the same, on the first Monday of July, and shall be a lien on said real estate from the fifteenth day of November, of the year in which such tax was assessed. [*Act of* 1869.]

Tax Roll for State and County purposes.

(§114.) SEC. 12. When the annual assessment roll shall have been examined, corrected, equalized and confirmed by the board of review, as provided in section six of this title, it shall be the duty of the Assessor to make copies of said rolls, by wards, as finally confirmed, and certify to the same, and retain the same until after the equalization thereof by the Board of Supervisors of Saginaw county; and said rolls are hereby determined and made the assessment rolls of the several wards of said city, for State and County purposes, upon which the Assessor shall ratably assess the State and County taxes certified to him from the board of supervisors of Saginaw county, adding thereto four per cent. for collector's fees,[a] at the same time, and in the same manner as township supervisors are or may be by law required to do; and when said rolls shall be completed, footed and balanced, the assessor shall deliver the same to the controller of said city, who shall annex thereto, a warrant authorizing and commanding the collection of the taxes thereon assessed, and the returns to be made to the county treasurer, in all respects as the same is or may be by law required in warrants of township treasurers, for the collection of taxes in the townships of this State. [*Act of* 1869.]

Common Council may borrow money.

(§115.) SEC. 13. For public improvements and building school-houses and other public buildings in said city, the common council may, if thereto authorized by a vote of the electors of said city, as provided in section two, title five, of this act, borrow on the faith

Note [a] See Amended Tax Law 1869.

of the city, a sum not exceeding one hundred and twenty-five thousand dollars, for a term not exceeding twenty years, at a rate of interest not exceeding ten per cent. per annum, payable annually, and for that purpose may issue bonds of the city, signed by the Mayor and Clerk, and countersigned by the Controller, and in such forms and sums, not exceeding in the aggregate the said sum of one hundred and twenty-five thousand dollars, as the said Common Council shall direct; and such bonds shall be disposed of under the direction of the Common Council of said city, upon such terms as they shall deem advisable, but not less than their par value, and the avails thereof shall be applied only for the purpose of public improvement and building school-houses and other public buildings in said city. But the Common Council may issue new bonds for the refunding of bonds and other evidences of debt, already issued, not exceeding twenty-five thousand dollars, in any one year, and for a term not exceeding twenty years, at a rate of interest not exceeding ten per cent. per annum, to be sold as above provided, the proceeds to be applied solely to paying existing indebtedness: *Provided*, The aggregate of bonds issued under authority of this section shall not at any one time, exceed the sum of one hundred and twenty-five thousand dollars. [*Act of* 1869.]

Limit of amount and terms.

Issue bonds.

How disposed of.

Common Council may re-issue Bonds for certain purposes.

(§116.) SEC. 14. It shall not be lawful for the Common Council, except as herein otherwise provided, to borrow any money or authorize the creation of any liability or indebtedness against said city in any one year, exceeding in the aggregate the amount which by this act may be raised by tax for such year, and in case any sum or sums of money shall be borrowed by said Common Council in any one year, or the said Common Council, or any officer thereof, shall enter into any contract or contracts for the payment of money binding upon said city, the same shall be paid out of the sums raised by tax for such year, if the payment thereof is not otherwise provided, and all sums of money borrowed by said city shall be applied to the purposes for which the same was borrowed, and for no other purpose whatsoever, but nothing in this act contained shall be construed to prohibit said Common Council from making assessments and levying and collecting taxes for the purpose of local improvements. [*Act of* 1865.]

Limitation of expenses to Annual Receipts.

(§117.) SEC 15. All sums of money directed to be raised by the Common Council, except as in this act otherwise provided,

Basis of Assessment.

shall be assessed upon all the real and personal estate in the said city, according to the valuation of the same as from the valuation thereof by the last preceeding assessment rolls filed in the office of the City Clerk; but no real or personal property which shall be exempt from taxation by the general laws of this State, nor any public square, park, or other public ground, shall be assessed for the ordinary city or county taxes. [*Act of* 1865.]

Exemptions

Sinking Fund; how levied, raised and collected

(§118.) SEC. 16. Whenever by the provisions of this act the Common Council shall be authorized to issue city bonds for the payment of any sum or sums of money, the said Common Council shall thereupon have the power to create a sinking fund for the payment of the interest as it falls due, and the extinguishment of the principal at the expiration of the time limited for the payment thereof, which fund shall be raised by a direct tax, which shall not exceed in any one year one half of one per cent. on the dollar on the valuation of the real and personal property within said city, and which shall be levied and collected in the same manner as the ordinary city taxes are levied and collected, but shall be put in a separate column in the tax roll, and when so collected, the same shall be applied to the credit of such sinking fund, for the purpose of paying off the principal and interest of the debt so created, as the same becomes due, and for no other purpose; and the fund so raised shall be securely invested in stocks of the United States or of this State, and said sinking fund shall not be used or borrowed for any other purpose than that for which it was raised. [*Act of* 1867.]

Money not to be drawn from Treasury except by appropriation.

(§ 119.) SEC. 17. No money shall be drawn from the City Treasury unless it shall have been previously appropriated to the purpose for which it shall be drawn; and all ordinances, resolutions and orders directing the payment of money, shall specify the object and purposes of such payment, which shall be certified by the Clerk, and countersigned by the Controller, before the same shall be paid by the Treasurer. [*Act of* 1865.]

Common Council have exclusive power to appropriate money.

(§ 120.) SEC. 18. The Common Council shall possess the exclusive power to appropriate moneys, and authorize the payment of claims and accounts chargeable against said corporation; but no unliquidated account or claim shall be allowed or received for audit by the Common Council or the Controller, unless it be ac.

companied by the affidavit of the person rendering it, or some person acquainted with the facts, to the effect that he verily believes that the services or property therein charged, have been actually performed or delivered to the city; that the sums charged therefor, are reasonable and just, and that to the best of his knowledge and belief, no setoff exists nor payment has been made on account thereof, except such as are included, or referred to in such account or claim. It shall be a sufficient bar or answer to any action or proceeding in any court for the collection of any demand or claim against said city, that it has never been presented to the Controller or Common Council for audit and allowance, or if so presented, was rejected for want of such affidavit, or that the action or proceeding was brought before the Common Council had a reasonable time to investigate and pass upon it. All amounts due upon contracts shall be audited according to the terms thereof, without unreasonable delay, but on the final settlement thereon, the contractor may be required to make the affidavit herein provided for, as in the case of other accounts. [*Act of* 1869.] Claims, how liquidated and audited.

(§ 121.) SEC. 19. The faith and property of the City of East Saginaw, shall remain pledged for the final payment of all bonds issued and all moneys borrowed by authority of or in accordance with this or any other act of the Legislature of this State. [*Act of* 1869.] Public faith pledged.

(§ 122.) SEC. 20. The Common Council may, whenever thereto authorized by vote of the electors of the city as provided in section two of this title, levy such tax in any one year or succession of years as the electors of said city, shall authorize, for the purpose of constructing a city hall, court house, prison, work-house or alms-houses. [*Act of* 1869.] Electors may vote tax for public buildings

TITLE VI.

OF STREETS AND PUBLIC IMPROVEMENTS.

Power of the Council over the Public Streets.

(§ 123.) SEC. 1. The Common Council of the City of East Saginaw shall have full power to lay out, establish, open, extend, widen, straighten, alter, close, fill in or grade, vacate or abolish any highways, streets, avenues, lanes, alleys, public grounds or spaces in said city, whenever they shall deem it a necessary public improvement, and private property may be taken therefor; but the necessity for using such property, the just compensation to be made for the same, shall be ascertained by a jury of twelve freeholders residing in said city, and it shall be and is hereby made the duty of the Common Council, within two years after this act takes effect, to establish and fix the grades for all streets in said city, and to have the same recorded in a book to be provided for that purpose, which book shall, at all times during reasonable hours be open to the inspection of all persons in said city. [*Act of* 1859]

Proceedings when private property is taken.

(§ 124.) SEC. 2. Whenever the Common Council shall deem any such improvement necessary, they shall so declare by resolution, which shall be drawn by the Attorney of the corporation, and said resolution shall describe the contemplated improvement; and if they intend to take private property therefor, they shall declare such intention, and describe such property in said resolution, with particularity sufficient for an ordinary conveyance thereof, and further declare that they will, on some day to be named in said resolution, apply to the Recorder's Court of said city, for the drawing of a jury to ascertain the necessity for using the property intended to be taken, if it be intended to take any for such improvement, to ascertain the just damages and compensation which any person may be entitled to if such intended improvement be made, and to apportion and assess such damages and compensation to and upon all lots, premises and subdivisions thereof, which will be benefitted by such improvement, and the time to be named for applying to said court shall be on a day subsequent to the required publication of said resolution. [*Act of* 1859.]

Council shall declare by resolution.

Application for a Jury.

(§ 125.) SEC. 3. The Common Council shall give notice of the intended improvement, and of the intended application to said court, by causing a copy of said resolution, certified by the Clerk of the city, to be published for four successive weeks, in some newspaper published in said city; and the Marshal shall also give notice of said resolution by delivering a notice thereof, with a copy of the same annexed, to the owner or owners of any property intended to be taken, if they can be found in said city, which notice

Resolution to be published.

Notice to the owner.

shall be directed to them; or, if they cannot be found in said city, by leaving the same at their place of residence in said city, with some person of proper age; if they or their place of residence cannot be found, and such property be occupied, said notice and copy of said resolution shall be served by delivering the same to the occupant or occupants, or by leaving the same at their place of residence within said city, with some person of proper age; but if the owner or owners of such property, or their place of residence cannot be found, and it be not occupied, or, if it be occupied, but they, their place of residence, and that of the occupant or occupants cannot be found, or if the owner or owners, occupant or occupants cannot be found, or if the owner or owners, occupant or occupants be unknown, or non-residents of said city, then, in either of such cases, notice of said resolution may be given by posting the same, with a copy of said resolution, in some conspicuous place upon the property intended to be taken; the Marshal shall give notice of said resolution, as above directed, and make return of his doings, and of the manner of giving said notice, as soon as practicable after the passage thereof, which return shall be made to the Recorder's Court at least six days before the day appointed in said resolution for the hearing of said application, and all persons interested therein, after notice given in the manner aforesaid, shall take notice of, and be bound by, all subsequent proceedings without any further notices, except as herein otherwise provided. [*Act of* 1859.]

Notice to non-residents.

Attorney to make application.

(§ 126.) SEC. 4. The Clerk of said city shall deliver to the attorney of the corportion, a certified copy of said resolution of the Common Council, whose duty it shall be to appear in said court, and make the application therein referred to, and conduct all further proceedings thereon in behalf of the Common Council. [*Act of* 1859.]

List of Jurors.

(§ 127.) SEC. 5. Upon the day designated in said resolution, or on some other day to be appointed by the court, and on filing a copy of said resolution, and an affidavit showing the required publication thereof, the Marshal shall attend said court, and write down the names of twenty-four disinterested freeholders residing in said city, and who shall be approved by the court, as such disinterested freeholders and residents, and qualified to serve. [*Act of* 1859.]

(§ 128.) SEC. 6. Said court shall then issue a summons, commanding the Marshal to summon said twenty-four persons to be and appear in said court to serve as jurors, on some day to be named therein, which shall not be less than seven days after the issuing thereof; the Marshal shall serve such summons at least three days before the return day thereof, and make return in the same manner as in the case of an ordinary venire for jurors of said court, and the persons thus summoned shall be bound to attend said court, and serve until discharged; and said court shall impose upon them a fine, not exceeding five dollars, for each day's non-attendance in court, or neglect to serve; but they may be exempted and excused by the court from serving, for the same reasons for which jurors in the circuit court may be exempted or excused. [*Act of* 1859.]

Summons for Jury.

Exemptions

(§ 129.) SEC. 7. The names of the jurors in attendance and who do not claim to be exempted, and are not excused from serving, shall then be written by the clerk of the court on separate slips of paper of equal size and appearance as near as practicable, and be deposited by him in a box having a lid or cover; he shall then shake said box so as thoroughly to mix said slips of paper, and shall then draw impartially, openly, and in presence of the court, so many of the slips of paper or ballots containing names written thereon, one after another, as shall be sufficient to form a jury. [*Act of* 1859.]

Drawing of Jury.

(§ 130.) SEC. 8. If, in consequence of jurors being exempted, excused or set aside, there shall not be in the box any slips or ballots, or not a sufficient number of ballots from which to draw the jury, the Marshal shall forthwith, under the order of the court, summons such number of persons as the court shall deem necessary, and may order to be and appear in said court to serve as jurors, and the persons thus summoned shall be returned, be bound to attend said court and serve, and be competent to form the jury in the same manner, and to the same effect, as those first summoned. [*Act of* 1859.]

Deficiency; how supplied.

(§ 131.) SEC. 9. The first twelve persons who shall appear as their names are drawn and called by the clerk, or who are called by him when all the ballots have been drawn from the jury box, and shall be approved by the court as qualified, shall be the jury,

Who to serve as Jurors.

and shall be sworn to discharge the duties imposed on them by this title, faithfully, impartially, and according to the best of their abilities; said court shall then instruct said jury as to their duties, and the law applicable to the case, and deliver to them a copy of the resolution of the Common Council as filed in said court, certified by the clerk thereof. [*Act of* 1859.]

Jury to view the Premises. (§ 132.) SEC. 10. Each of said jurors shall go to the place of the intended improvement, and upon or as near as practicable to any property intended to be taken and described in said resolution or as the case may be, which will be damaged or benefitted if the intended improvement be made. [*Act of* 1859.]

Necessity for using ascertained. (§ 133.) SEC. 11. Said jury shall then ascertain the necessity for using the property intended to be taken, if it be intended to take any for such improvement, the just damages and compensation to be paid to the owner or owners of any property intended to be taken for, and to award the owner or owners thereof such damages and compensation as they shall deem just. If such property shall be subject to a valid mortgage, lease, lien, levy or agreement, or to either, then said jury shall apportion and award to the owner or owners of such property, the parties in interest to such mortgage, lease, lien, levy or agreement, or to either of them, such portions of the damage and compensation as they shall deem just. [*Act of* 1859.]

Apportion and Assess damages. (§ 134.) SEC. 12. Said jury shall then apportion and assess the total damages and compensation to be paid in any case to and upon all lots of land, premises or subdivisions thereof, which will be benefitted if the intended improvement be made, apportioning and assessing to and upon each, such portion of said total damages and compensation as they shall deem just: *Provided, however,* That if the total damages and compensation to be awarded to any person or persons as above shall exceed the total benefits to be apportioned to and assessed upon any property for the benefit such property will receive, then such excess shall be apportioned and assessed to the city of East Saginaw. [*Act of* 1859.]

Proviso.

Report of Jury. (§ 135.) SEC. 13. Said jury shall then make, in writing, and each shall sign a report to said court of their doings, enclose the same in a sealed envelope, and file it in the office of the clerk of said court, within ten days after they were sworn. [*Act of* 1859.]

(§ 136.) SEC. 14. Said jury shall state in their report the just damages and compensation ascertained and awarded by them to the owner of any private property, or to any person claiming an interest therein by virtue of any mortgage, lease, lien, levy or agreement, or either, to which such property may be subject, together with the name of such owner or claimant, if known, and a description of the property intended to be taken. In case any damage and compensation be awarded to any person claiming an interest in such property by virtue of any valid mortgage, lease, lien, levy or agreement, or either, to which such property may be subject, it shall be sufficient to state further, in such case, the name of such interested party, the date of such mortgage, lease, lien, levy or agreement, or assignment thereof, if there be any, by virtue of which such interested party has an interest in the property intended to be taken. [*Act of* 1859.]

What Report shall state.

(§ 137.) SEC. 15. Said jury shall also state in their report what portions in amount of the total ascertained damages and compensation they have apportioned to and assessed upon any lot, premises, or subdivision thereof, which will be benefitted by the intended improvement, together with the names of the owners thereof, if known, and a description of the same, and also what portion, if any, of the ascertained damages and compensation, they have apportioned and assessed to the city of East Saginaw, in the case above provided for. [*Act of* 1859.]

Ibid.

(§ 138.) SEC. 16. Said report may be confirmed by said court at any term thereof, or at any time when said court may be regularly in session; and the said court shall appoint some day when it will consider said report, and objections against the confirmation thereof on the part of all persons interested therein, whereof the City Attorney shall give notice by publishing the same in some newspaper published in said city for one week, and he shall file in said court an affidavit of such publication before the time appointed for considering said report; said objections shall be filed with the Clerk in writing, but may be argued, and the consideration of said report and objections may be adjourned from time to time, until said report be confirmed or otherwise disposed of, as herein provided. [*Act of* 1859.]

Confirmation of Report.

Objections to Report.

Basis of Objections.

(§ 139.) SEC. 17. Said report shall not be annulled for objections as to matters of form; all objections shall be objections of law, and to matters of substance; but the damages and compensation to be paid to any person, or the portions thereof, apportioned thereto or assessed upon any lot of land, premises, or subdivision thereof, may be enquired into, if objected to as being excessively large or small. [*Act of* 1859.]

Further Proceedings

(§ 140.) SEC. 18. If no objections be filed, said report shall be confirmed; but if objections be filed, said court, after considering the same, and after argument thereon, shall in its discretion, confirm or annul said report, or may refer it back to the same jury, for the purpose of reviewing all matters and correcting all errors therein contained, and making any alterations thereof which said court may direct, or said jury may deem just or necessary; and thereon said jury shall review, correct or alter said report, in manner aforesaid, and shall return and file the same with the clerk of said court, within five days after said report was referred back to them as aforesaid, and thereupon said court shall confirm or annul said report. [*Act of* 1859.]

Provides for new Jury.

(§ 141.) SEC. 19. If said report be annulled, or the jury cannot agree, or from death, sickness, or any other cause, shall fail to make a report within the ten days required above, the court may, on the application of the Attorney, designate some day in term when another jury may be had, and such jury shall be obtained, drawn, summoned, returned, bound to attend and serve, have the same qualifications, be sworn, and when sworn, have the same powers and duties as the first jury; the same proceedings, after they are sworn, shall be had by them, and by and in said court, as provided for above, after the first jury is sworn. [*Act of* 1859.]

Disability of Jurors.

(§ 142.) SEC. 20. If any juror, after being sworn, shall die or from sickness be unable to discharge his duties, the court may appoint another person to serve in his place, who shall be sworn, and shall have the like qualifications, powers and duties as those already sworn. [*Act of* 1859.]

Right of Appeal.

(§ 143.) SEC. 21. Any person to whom damages and compensation may be awarded for any of his property intended to be taken, or on account of the intended improvement, or to and upon whose property any portion of such damages and compensation may be apportioned and assessed, considering himself aggrieved, may appeal from the judgment of the Recorder's Court confirming the report of the jury to the Supreme Court, by filing in writing with the clerk of said Recorder's Court a notice of such appeal and specification of the errors complained of, within five days after the confirmation, and serving within the same time a copy of said notice and specification of errors on the Attorney of the corporation, and filing a bond in said Recorder's Court, to be approved by the Recorder, conditioned for the prosecution of said appeal, and the payment of all costs that may be awarded against the appellant, in case the judgment of confirmation of the Recorder's Court be affirmed. [*Act of* 1859.]

Duty of Clerk.

(§ 144.) SEC. 22. In case of appeal as above, it shall be the duty of the clerk of the Recorder's Court forthwith, or as soon as practicable, to transmit to the Supreme Court a certified copy of all the proceedings in the case, which may be filed in the office of any clerk of said Supreme Court. [*Act of* 1859.]

Proceedings on Appeal.

(§ 145.) SEC. 23. The Supreme Court, at any term thereof, shall with the least practicable delay, hear and try the matter of said appeal, and may affirm or reverse the judgmeut of the Recorder's Court confirming the report of the jury; but the same shall not be reversed for matter of form, nor for any errors except errors of law, and only in regard to the appellant or appellants. The court shall give judgment for reasonable costs and expenses in the matter of said appeal and proceedings thereon, to be taxed, and all costs and expenses awarded to the City of East Saginaw in case of affirmation, shall be applied on and deducted from the damages and compensation, if any, to be paid to the appellant or appellants. [*Act of* 1859.]

Proceedings remanded for correction.

(§ 146.) SEC. 24. If there be a reversal for any errors which it is practicable for the Recorder's Court or said jury to correct, with due regard to the public interest and rights of individuals, the proceedings shall be remanded to said Recorder's Court, with directions that such errors be corrected. Said Recorder's Court, at any term thereof, or (as the case may be) said jury, under the direction of said court, shall correct such error, and thereupon the report of the jury shall be confirmed by said Recorder's Court, without any further right of appeal. [*Act of* 1859.]

Proceedings in case of amendment. (§ 147.) SEC. 25. In case of every annullment of the report of the jury by the Recorder's court, or reversal by the Supreme Court, the Common Council, in behalf of said city may, by resolution, elect to pay the damages and compensation claimed by, or the assessment made upon the property of the objector, appellant or appellants, on filing a certified copy of said resolution in the Recorder's court, within twenty days after the annulment or reversal, the report of said jury shall be reviewed and confirmed by said Recorder's court, as to all persons interested therein, except the objector, appellant or appellants, and without further right of appeal. If the Common Council do not elect as above provided, all the proceedings shall be null and void, and no further proceedings shall be had, except in case of reversal, when the proceedings may have been remanded to the Recorder's court, for the correction of certain errors, in which case, such errors shall be corrected, and the report of the jury confirmed, as above provided. [*Act of* 1859.]

Confirmation to be final. (§ 148.) SEC. 26. If the report of the jury be confirmed by the Recorder's court, in any case above provided for, or if the judgment of confirmation be affirmed, on appeal to the Supreme Court, such confirmation shall be final and conclusive, as to all persons interested therein; and the damages and compensation apportioned to and assessed upon any lot of land, premises, or subdivision thereof, according to said report, as confirmed, shall be a lien thereon, from the time of the aforesaid confirmation until they are paid and satisfied. [*Act of* 1859.]

Copy to be filed with the City Clerk (§ 149.) SEC. 27. When the report of the jury shall have thus been finally confirmed, or the judgment of confirmation affirmed by the Supreme Court, the Clerk of the Recorder's court shall prepare a certified copy, under the seal of the court, of the report of the jury as confirmed by the Recorder's court, and of the order of the court confirming the same, and the Clerk shall file said certified copy in the office of the Clerk of the city, who shall record the same in a book to be provided, used and known as a book of street records. Such certified copy, such record, or a like copy made and certified by the Clerk of the Recorder's court, shall, in all courts and places be presumptive evidence of the matters therein contained, and of the regularity of all proceedings from the commencement thereof to the order of the court confirming the report of the jury. [*Act of* 1859.]

(§ 150.) SEC. 28. The amounts apportioned to, and assessed upon all lots of land, premises, or subdivisions thereof, for the benefits they will receive, shall be paid to the Treasurer of said city, in case of confirmation of the report of the jury as above provided, or in case the judgment of confirmation be affirmed by the Supreme Court, and warrant or warrants authorizing the collection thereof shall be issued as soon as practicable, under the hand of the Mayor and the corporate seal of the city, directed to the Marshal thereof, and in the collection of such assessments the said Marshal shall proceed in the same manner, and shall levy, collect, make return to the City Clerk of the sums remaining uncollected, with a description of the lots, premises or subdivisions, parts or portions thereof, upon which such tax was assessed, and which remains unpaid as aforesaid, and the City Clerk shall report the same to the Controller, who shall assess the same upon the assessment and tax roll upon such premises, and the same shall be thereupon collected and returned, and the same proceedings had for the collection and return thereof, and for the sale of such premises for the non-payment of such assessment and the charges accruing thereon, as is provided by this act in the case of the collection of assessments made for public improvements in said city. [*Act of* 1859.]

Assessm'ts, to whom paid.

Warrants for the collection of same.

(§ 151.) SEC. 29. Within three months after the confirmation of the report of the jury, or after the judgment of confirmation shall, on appeal, be affirmed, the Common Council shall pay or tender to the respective persons the several amounts of damages and compensation awarded to them, according to the report of the jury as confirmed, or elected, as above provided for, to be paid by the Common Council; and in case any such person shall refuse the same, be unknown, or a non-resident of said city, or from any reason incapacitated from receiving his or her amount, or the right thereto to be disputed or doubtful. the Common Council may deposit the amount awarded in such case, or elected to be paid by the Common Council, in the treasury of the city, to the credit of any person entitled thereto, and shall, on demand, pay the same over to any person or persons competent and entitled to

Common Council shall pay or tender damages.

Deposit in certain cases.

receive it, and the Treasurer shall take receipt and voucher therefor. [*Act of* 1859.]

When title to vest in city.

(§ 152.) SEC. 30. Upon such payment, tender or deposit in the City Treasury, the fee and ownership of the land and property to be taken, shall be fully vested in the said city, and the Common Council may enter upon, take possession of, and convert the same to the uses and purposes for which it has been taken. A certificate of the City Treasurer of such tender, payment or deposit, or record thereof in the book of street records, or certified copy of such record, shall, in all courts and places, be presumptive evidence of the facts therein stated, of the vesting of the fee of the property taken in the City of East Saginaw, and of the right of the Common Council to take possession and convert the same to the uses for which it has been taken. [*Act of* 1859.]

Proceedings when property taken is encumbered.

(§ 153.) SEC. 31. In all cases where any real estate, subject to any lease or agreement, shall be taken as aforesaid, all the covenants and stipulations contained therein shall cease, determine, and be discharged, upon the final confirmation of the report of the jury, or upon the affirmation, by the Supreme Court, of the judgment of confirmation. If a part only of such real estate be taken, said covenants and stipulations shall cease, determine and be discharged, only as to such part; and the Recorder's Court, on application of any party in interest to such lease or agreement, and after a notice thereof of eight days, in writing, to the other parties in interest, may appoint three disinterested residents and freeholders of said city, commissioners to determine the rents and payments (to be) thereafter paid, and the covenants, stipulations or conditions thereafter to be performed under the lease or agreement, in respect to the residue or part of such real estate not taken. Said Commissioners shall, before entering on their duties, take and subscribe an oath, to be administered by the court, faithfully to discharge their duties, which oath shall be filed in said court. Said three Commissioners shall make and sign a report in writing, of their doings to said court, which shall be filed therein within thirty days after their appointment; and said report on being confirmed by the court, shall be binding and conclusive on the parties in interest to such lease or agreement, and the fees and expenses of proceedings under this section shall be borne in

Commissioners.

Duties.

whole or in part by the parties to such lease or agreement, or either of them or by the City of East Saginaw, in the discretion of the Common Council. [*Act of* 1859.]

(§ 154.) SEC. 32. The duties above in this title to be performed by the Marshal of said city, excepting the collection of the assessments by virtue of section twenty-eight, in case of the inability of such Marshal, whether by absence, sickness, or interest in the subject matter of the proceedings, may be performed by either of the Ward Constables of said city. [*Act of* 1859.]

Duties of Marshal may be performed by Constable.

(§ 155.) SEC. 33. The Common Council shall pay said jury such compensation for their services as they may deem just, and they shall have power to abandon or discontinue proceedings under this chapter in said Recorder's Court, at any time before the final confirmation of the report of the jury. [*Act of* 1859.]

Compensation to Jury

May abandon proceedings.

(§ 156.) SEC. 34. The Common Council shall be Commissioners of highways of said city, and shall have the care and supervision of the highways, streets, bridges, lanes, alleys, parks and public grounds therein; and it shall be their duty to give directions for the repairing, preserving, improving, cleansing and securing of such highways, bridges, lanes, alleys, parks and public grounds, and to cause the same to be repaired, cleansed, improved and secured, from time to time, as may be necessary; to regulate the roads, streets, highways, lanes, parks and alleys already laid out, or which may hereafter be laid out, and to alter such of them as they shall deem inconvenient, subject to the restrictions contained in this title; to cause such of the streets and highways in said city as shall have been used for six years or more as public highways and streets, and which are not sufficiently described, or have not been duly recorded, to be ascertained, described, and recorded in the office of the City Clerk of said city, in the book of street records; and the recording of such highways, streets, lanes, alleys or public grounds, so ascertained and described, or which shall hereafter be laid out and established by said Common Council, and recorded in the book of street records, in the office of the clerk, by order of the Common Council, shall be presumptive evidence of the existence of such highway, street, lane, alley or public ground, therein described; to divide said city from time to time, into so many highway districts as they shall deem expedient, by

General Power of Council as to streets.

an ordinance or resolution entered upon their minutes; to appoint and assign to each of such districts so many inspectors of streets, as they shall from time to time deem proper, and such Inspectors shall in all cases, when required by the Common Council, give such securities as said Council shall require, for the faithful performance of their duties; and the Council may assign to said Inspectors such duties in relation to the opening, laying out, making, repairing and preserving the streets, highways, lanes, alleys, parks, squares and public grounds of said city, as they may deem expedient; and the said Inspectors shall possess all the powers and be subject to all the liabilities of Overseers of Highways in the several townships, of the State, so far as the same may be applicable to said city under the provisions of this act. [*Act of* 1859.]

Power to construct Sewers, &c. (§ 157.) SEC. 35. The Common Council shall have power to cause common sewers, drains and vaults, arches and bridges, wells, pumps and reservoirs to be built in any part of said city; to cause the grading raising, leveling, repairing, amending, paving or covering with broken or pounded stone, plank or other material, any street, lane, alley, highway, public ground or sidewalk of said city. [*Act of* 1859.]

Discontinuing of streets (§ 158.) SEC. 36. The Common Council shall have the same power in relation to discontinuing any street, highway, lane or alley in said city, which the commissioners of highways in townships have or may hereafter receive in relation to town highways, and they may adopt the same proceedings to affect such object as near as may be, as the commissioners of highways in townships are or may be by law required to adopt, and appeals may be taken to the Recorder's court in like manner as far as practicable, as appeals are now or may hereafter by law be taken from the decisions of highway commissioners in townships, and the said Recorder's court is hereby authorized and empowered to hear and determine such appeals. [*Act of* 1859.]

Proceedings when expense is to be assessed on propety benefitted. (§ 159.) SEC. 37. Whenever the Common Council shall determine that the whole or any part of the expenses of any public improvement not requiring the taking of any land by the said city, shall be defrayed by an assessment on the owners or occupants of houses and lands to be benefitted thereby, they shall declare the same by an entry in their minutes, and cause the necessary plans, profiles and specifications to be made, and proceed to advertise and let the contract for the performance of said work to the lowest responsible bidder therefor; and the Common Council shall also declare, by resolution, whether the whole or what portion of the cost of such improvement shall be assessed to such owners and occupants; and the Common Council shall further declare and set forth by resolution, to be entered upon the proceedings, all lots, blocks and parcels of real estate, or parts thereof, which in their opinion, will be benefitted thereby, and which shall be assessed therefor, which resolution shall be printed in at least one newspaper published in said city, at least once prior to the ordering of any assessment thereon; and the owner or occupant of any property so mentioned and set forth, if he shall feel injured or aggrieved thereby, or shall take any exception thereto, shall appear at the next regular meeting of the Common Council, and object; and the Common Council shall hear and determine upon such objection, but if such owner or occupant shall fail so to appear, or if the Common Council shall, after hearing the objections, refuse to change such designation, the same shall be final. [*Act of* 1869.]

Owner may object.

(§ 160.) SEC. 38. The Common Council shall thereupon and thereafter, make an order reciting the public improvement to be made, the estimated amount of the expense to be assessed as aforesaid, including the cost and expenses of making estimates, plans, assessments, and other expenses incidental thereto, not including interest, which estimate shall be made by the City Surveyor, and filed in the office of the Controller, and the description of property on which the same is to be assessed. [*Act of* 1869.]

Expense ascertained.

(§ 161.) SEC. 39. The City Clerk shall, within one week after the making of such order, certify a copy of the same, under seal, to the assessor of said city, who shall proceed without unnecessary delay, to make an assessment, according to such order, and make out an assessment roll, reciting in the heading thereof the improvement ordered, and in the body of which shall be entered the names of the persons assessed, a description of the property, and the amount or amounts, in dollars and cents, assessed thereon: *Provided*, In all cases where the property designated shall be vacant and unoccupied, and the ownership thereof unknown to the assessor, he shall insert in lieu of the name of said owner, the word "non-resident." [*Act of* 1869.]

Assessment how to be made.

Certificate. (§ 162.) SEC. 40. The assessor shall certify upon such roll that he has made said assessment upon the persons and property described, in accordance with the order of the Common Council relating thereto, and that the said roll contains a just and true assessment of the costs of such improvement, (stating the sum thereof,) and that the several amounts assessed against each person and description of property has been set down, as nearly as may be, and to the best of his judgment, according to the benefit and advantage which such person or description of property is by him deemed to acquire from the making of said improvement. [*Act of* 1869.]

Duty of Clerk. (§ 163.) SEC. 41. As soon as said roll is completed and certified to, the assessor shall file the same with the City Clerk, who shall letter it as "special assessment roll, (using the letters of the alphabet in their order,) for the year 18—," and also endorse the date when so filed thereon, and report the same to the Common Council at its next meeting. [*Act of* 1869.]

Notice to be given on completion of Roll. (§ 164.) SEC. 42. Upon such notice of the completion of such assessment, and filing of any special assessment roll, the Common Council shall cause notice to be given to all parties interested therein, reciting the names on said roll, by publication in a newspaper published in said city, for at least two weeks, that the Common Council will, at such time as they shall appoint, hear objections to, and appeals from said assessment. [*Act of* 1869.]

Proceedings thereon. (§ 165.) SEC. 42. At the time appointed for that purpose, and such other times as the hearing shall be adjourned to, the Common Council shall hear the allegations and proofs of all persons who may complain of such assessment, and may rectify and amend the said assessment in whole or in part, or may set the same aside and direct a new assessment, or the said Common Council may ratify and confirm such assessment without any corrections or with such conditions therein, as they may think proper. [*Act of* 1869.]

Confirmation final. Tax a legal charge. (§ 166.) SEC. 44. Every assessment so ratified and confirmed shall be final and conclusive, and the same shall become a legal charge against the persons named therein; and within five days after the same shall be confirmed, the Controller shall deliver the same to the City Treasurer, and give public notice thereof by advertisement in the official paper of the city, for at least one week, and the said Treasurer shall give a receipt for said roll, and be charged therewith, and shall retain the same in his office for the space of sixty days, during which time any person may pay the amount of taxes against such person or his property respectively to said Treasurer, who shall receive said taxes and give a receipt therefor, and mark the same paid upon the roll; and within five days after the expiration of the time for the payment of said assessment to the Treasurer as aforesaid, the Controller shall take such assessment roll into his hands, and shall add four per cent. as fees for collecting the same, and shall annex or attach a warrant to said special assessment roll, directed to any Ward Collector of the city, which warrant shall be signed by the Controller, and have the city seal stamped thereon, which warrant shall command said Collector to collect the taxes unpaid upon said roll within the time prescribed in said warrant; and such Collector shall thereupon be authorized and required to levy and collect the same by distress and sale of any personal property of the person chargeable with such tax; and in case sufficient personal property cannot be found whereon to levy and collect such tax, the Collector shall, within five days after the time prescribed by his said warrant for the collection thereof has expired, pay to the City Treasurer all sums collected on such tax roll, and make report to the Controller of the sums so paid, and of all assessments thereon remaining unpaid, which he was unable, for want of such personal property, to levy and collect of the same, together with the description of the premises assessed for such unpaid taxes, which return shall, in all cases, be made under oath, and shall be filed and preserved in the office of the Controller. Upon the filing of such return by the Collector, thereupon such unpaid taxes shall become a lien upon the real estate described on said roll; and the taxes assessed thereon shall draw interest at the rate of twenty per cent. per annum as hereinafter provided; but any person owning any premises so chargeable with such special assessment or tax, may discharge such premises from such tax at any time after such return by the Collector, and before it is put into the general city roll as hereinafter provided, by paying to the City Treasurer the amount of tax so assessed against him or his property, together with the interest at the rate of twenty per cent. per annum from the time of the return by the Collector of such roll to the date of such payment. On or before the first day of June succeeding, the Controller shall certify to

Collection of Tax.

Duty of Controller.

Duty of Collector.

Become a lien. Interest.

Owner may redeem.

Delinquent Taxes returned to Assessor and placed on city roll.

the Assessor the amount of such taxes, and the description of the premises assessed and chargable with such tax, who shall assess such unpaid taxes, together with interest, at the rate of twenty per cent. on all sums so uncollected and unpaid, from the date of the return of such assessment and tax roll by the Collector, to the first day of August in the year in which the same shall be placed by the Assessor, as herein provided, on such premises in the tax roll next thereafter to be made, and such tax shall then be levied, collected and returned, and the said premises may be sold for non-payment thereof, as provided by law for the non-payment of other taxes. [*Act of* 1869.]

Who shall be liable for Tax.

(§ 167.) SEC. 45. In cases where there is no agreement to the contrary, the owner or landlord, and not the occupant or tenant, shall be deemed in law the person who ought to bear and pay every such assessment, made for the expense of any public improvement in the said city. [*Act of* 1859.]

Right to recover.

(§ 168.) SEC. 46. Where any such assessment shall be made upon or paid by any person, when by agreement or by law the same ought to be borne or paid by any other person, it shall be lawful for the one so paying to sue for and recover of the person bound to pay the same the amount so paid, with interest. [*Act of* 1859.]

Agreements not affected.

(§ 169.) SEC. 47. Nothing herein contained shall impair, or in any way effect, any agreement between any landlord and tenant, or other persons, respecting the payment of any such assessments. [*Act of* 1859.]

Excess of Tax, how disposed of.

(§ 170.) SEC. 48. If, upon completion of any such improvement, for which such assessment shall have been made, it shall appear that a greater amount has been assessed and collected than is necessary to defray the expenses thereof, the Common Council shall apportion such excess among the persons and property assessed, in proportion to the amount collected of them, and shall pay the same to such persons, and the owner of such property entitled thereto, on demand. [*Act of* 1859.]

Deficiency, how supplied.

(§ 171.) SEC. 49. If it appear that a greater sum of money has been expended, in the completion of such improvement, than was estimated as aforesaid, the Common Council may direct the assessment of the same on the owners and occupants of houses and lands benefitted by such improvements, in the same manner as herein above directed, and the same proceedings, in all respects, shall be had thereon, and the Common Council may enlarge the territory to be assessed for such improvements. [*Act of* 1859.]

Territory enlarged.

(§ 172.) SEC. 50. The term public improvement, as used in this act, shall be held and construed to include, not only those set out and recited in the first section of this title, but the stumping, ditching and grading of all public streets, highways, lanes and alleys; the construction of plank roads, the laying of pavements of wood or stone, including the cross-walk, flagging, and curbing, excavating and grading for the same; the planking, graveling or macadamizing, with broken or pounded stone, of the streets or road-ways of said city; the draining and filling of all low lands and lots, and the general betterment of all streets, highways, lanes, alleys, parks, public places and grounds within said city. All proceedings of the Common Council, under the provisions of this title, shall be matters of record in the proceedings of the Common Council, and shall not fail on account of any technical or clerical error made by any officer of the city, and shall be construed favorably by all courts of the State for any beneficial purpose therein and thereby intended; and in any case of litigation, suit or injunction that may arise between the corporation and any person, out of proceedings under this title, the court shall require the complainant to furnish sufficient bonds and sureties to indemnify the city against any loss or damage that may accrue to it from such proceedings, before granting process or injunction against the said corporation. [*Act of* 1869.]

Public improvement shall be construed, to include, &c.

Record not void on account of clerical errors.

Construed favorably.

Complainant to give security to the city.

(§ 173.) SEC. 51. Whenever the Common Council shall deem it expedient to construct any side-walk of plank, or other material on any street within the said city, they may, by ordinance, or otherwise, require the owner, or occupant of any lot or house adjoining such street to construct such sidewalk on such street, in front of his or her lot or house; or they may direct such side-walks to be made according to the provisions of this title. The Common Council may, in like manner, by ordinance or otherwise, under such penalty or penalties as they may prescribe, require the

Side-Walks how to be constructed, &c.

Repairs, &c.

owners and occupants, or either, of land in said city, or in any specified part thereof, to repair, maintain and re-construct side-walks, pavements and street improvements, adjoining their respective premises, to the middle of the street or alley, the expense to be defrayed by assessment, in such manner as the Common Council, by ordinance or otherwise, may direct; the expense to which any occupant or tenant may thus be subjected, may be collected by him from the owner of the premises, unless otherwise agreed, or unless such tenant or occupant be bound to bear such expense by the terms or nature of the agreement under which he holds the premises. [*Act of* 1869.]

Orders and Ordinances, how enforced.

(§ 174.) SEC. 52. Whenever the owner or occupant of any lot or house shall refuse or neglect, within such time as the Common Council shall have appointed, to conform to any regulation made by the said Common Council for widening streets, or for any other purpose, it shall be lawful for the said Common Council to cause such regulations to be enforced at the expense of the city, and to recover the amount of such expenses with damages, at the rate of ten per centum, with costs of suit, from the owner or occupant of such lot, or house, whose duty it was to conform to such regulations: *Provided*, That the Council may, in all such cases, elect to assess the amount so to be paid upon the lot or lots to be benefited by such improvement or regulation, or for building any plank or other side-walk, and when such assessment shall be duly levied and confirmed, the same may be collected in the same manner provided by section forty-four of this title. [*Act of* 1859.]

Proviso.

Assess non-residents for repairs, &c.

(§ 175.) SEC. 53. The Common Council are authorized to assess the lands of non-residents of said city, their just proportion of the expenses of cleaning and repairing streets and side-walks, and removing nuisances, and the said expenses shall be assessed in the same manner, and the amount so assessed shall be collected in the same manner, and the same proceedings shall be had in case of non-payment of the same, as in relation to the assessments for public improvements in said city; except as the Common Council may otherwise determine or direct. [*Act of* 1859.]

Drain or Sewer Assessment.

(§ 176.) SEC. 54. The Common Council shall have full power to assess and collect of each individual using or being benefited by any public sewer or drain, as follows, to wit: The sum of ten dollars for making connection with any such drain or sewer, and the further sum of two dollars and fifty cents annually for each cellar drained, directly or indirectly, by a drain, into any public drain or sewer, which assessment shall be taken to include all other drainage of the premises to which said cellar especially belongs; and the sum of two dollars annually for each lot or subdivision of lot being without a cellar, drained as aforesaid, into any public drain or sewer, and such sums as may be fixed by the Common Council for all establishments requiring an unusual or extraordinary amount of drainage, drained as aforesaid; which sums shall, with the names of such individuals and the description of such lands or premises, liable to pay the same, be reported annually, on or before the last Saturday in May, in each year, by the Board of Sewer Commissioners to the Assessor, who shall assess the same upon such persons and lands, and place the same in the annual tax roll, in the sewer column, and the same shall be enforced and collected in the same manner as general taxes of said city, and shall go into the sewer fund, and shall be expended exclusively for the repairs and construction of sewers.[a] [*Act of* 1869.]

Collection of Assessments, &c.

(§ 177.) SEC. 55. When any assessment for public improvements, or any local improvements, or expenses upon any ward, highway district, street, lane, alley, public sewer or other improvement shall have been made, as in this act provided and shall be confirmed by the Common Council, it shall become a charge against the person assessed, and the same proceedings shall be had for collecting the same as is provided in section forty-four of this title; and when said rolls shall be returned to the Controller, the said assessments unpaid shall thereupon become a lien upon the real estate described upon said roll, subject to the same rate of interest and terms of payment as other special assessment rolls hereinbefore provided; and they shall be, by the Controller in a like manner, returned or certified to the Assessor, who shall assess the same upon the annual assessment and tax roll, upon such premises, and the same shall be thereupon collected and returned, and the same proceedings had for the collection and return thereof, and for the

---

See Sec. Title 12.

sale of such premises for the non-payment of such tax or assessment as is provided by law for the collection and return and sale of premises for non-payment of the ordinary city taxes. [*Act of* 1869.]

Sale of personal property by Collectors.

(§ 178.) SEC. 56. When any Collector shall have levied on personal property for the non-payment of any tax or assessment, in this act provided, he shall proceed to advertise and sell the same, in the same manner, and upon like notice, and make return of all money received therefrom, as is or may be required by the general laws of this State, in the levy and sale of personal property for non-payment of taxes by township treasurers. [*Act of* 1869]

Owner or Agent allowed to make improvements

(§ 179.) SEC. 57. The Common Council shall permit any person who shall be the owner or agent of any tract, plat or addition, within the limits of said city, to improve, grade, plank or pave any street lying within said tract, plat or addition, the cost of which, if improved by the order of the Council, could be assessed against such person or agent, upon request: *Provided*, All such work shall be done under the superintendence of the Street Commissioner and City Surveyor, and shall, in all respects, conform to the established plan and grades for streets in said city. [*Act of* 1869.]

Re-Assessments. Power of Council and how made.

(§ 180.) SEC. 58. Whenever any special assessment for the improvement of a street, or for any other public work, shall, in the opinion of the Common Council, be deemed invalid, said Common Council may vacate and set the same aside; and when any such special assessment shall be so vacated, or shall be held invalid by the judgment or decree of any court of competent jurisdiction, said Common Council may cause a new assessment to be made. Such new assessment shall be made in the manner provided for making original assessments of like nature, and whenever the tax or any part thereof, assessed upon any lot or parcel of real estate by the original assessment has been paid and shall not have been refunded, it shall be the duty of the Assessor and Controller to apply said assessment upon the re-assessment upon said lot or parcel, and to make a minute thereof upon the new assessment roll, and such re-assessment shall be deemed paid and satisfied. All the provisions of this charter [act] making special assessments a charge against the persons assessed, or a lien upon the lots and parcels of real estate embraced therein, and also those relating to the collection and return of special assessments, shall in like manner apply to such re-assessment. [*Act of* 1869.]

TITLE VII.

FIRE DEPARTMENT—PREVENTION AND EXTINGUISHMENT OF FIRES, FIRE LIMITS, &C.

Powers as to fires. Buildings Fire limits, &c. Penalty.

(§ 181.) SEC. 1. For the purpose of guarding against the calamities of fire, the Common Council may, from time to time, by ordinance, designate such portions and parts of the said city as they shall think proper, within which no buildings of wood shall be erected; and may regulate and direct the erection of buildings within such portions and parts, and the size and materials thereof, and the size of the chimneys therein; and every person who shall violate any such ordinance or regulation shall forfeit to the city the sum of one hundred dollars; and every building erected contrary to such ordinance is hereby declared to be a common nuisance, and may be abated and removed by such Common Council. [*Act of* 1859.]

Construct'n of buildings

(§ 182.) SEC. 2. The Common Council may, by ordinance, require the owners and occupants of houses and other buildings to have scuttles on the roofs of such houses and buildings, and stairs or ladders leading to the same; and whenever any penalty shall have been recovered against the owner or occupant of any house or other building for not complying with such ordinance, the Common Council may, at the expiration of twenty days after such recovery, cause such scuttles and stairs or ladders to be constructed, and may recover the expense thereof, with ten per cent. in addition, of the owner or occupant whose duty it was to comply with such ordinance. [*Act of* 1859.]

(§ 183.) SEC. 3. The Common Council may regulate and direct the construction of safe deposits for ashes, and may compel the clearing of chimneys, flues, stovepipes, and all other conductors of smoke, and upon the neglect of the owner or occupant of any house, tenement, or building of any description, having therein any chimneys, flues, stovepipes, or other conductors of smoke, to clean the same, as shall have been directed by any ordinance, the Common Council may cause the same to be cleaned, and may collect the expense thereof, and ten per cent. in addition, from the owner or occupant whose duty it was to have the same cleaned. [*Act of* 1859.]

Stove pipes, chimneys, ashes, &c.

(§ 184.) SEC. 4. The Common Council may regulate the use of lights and candles in livery stables and other buildings in which combustible articles may be deposited, and may prescribe the use of lanterns or safety lamps in such buildings, and may regulate the transporting, keeping and deposit of gunpowder or other dangerous or combustible materials, and may prevent or regulate the carrying on of manufactories dangerous in causing or promoting fires, and may authorize and direct the removal of any hearth, fire-place, stovepipe, flue, chimney, or other conductor of smoke, or any other apparatus or device in which any fire may be used, or to which fire may be applied, that shall be considered dangerous, and liable to cause and promote fires, and generally may adopt such other regulations for the prevention and suppression of fires, as they may deem necessary. [*Act of* 1859.]

Lamps.

Gunpowder &c.

(§ 185.) SEC. 5. For the purpose of enforcing such regulations, the Common Council may authorize any of the officers of the said city, and may appoint persons at all reasonable times, to enter into and examine all dwelling houses, buildings and tenements of every description, and all lots, yards and enclosures, and to cause such as are dangerous to be put in safe condition, and may authorize such officers and persons to inspect all hearths, fireplaces, stoves,

May appoint Inspectors, &c.

pipes, flues, chimneys, or other conductors of smoke, or any apparatus or device in which fire may be used, or to which fire may be applied, and remove and make the same safe, at the expense of the owners or occupants of the buildings in which the same may be, and to ascertain the situation of any building in respect to its exposure to fire, and whether any scuttles and ladders thereto have been provided, and generally, with such powers and duties as the Common Council shall deem necessary, to guard the city from the calamities of fire. [*Act of* 1859.]

Fire Engines, &c. (§ 186.) SEC. 6. The Common Council may procure, own, build, erect and keep in repair, such and so many fire-engines, with their hose and other apparatus, engine-houses, ladders, fire-hooks and fire buckets, and other implements and conveniences for the extinguishment of fires, and to prevent injuries by fire, and such and so many public cisterns, wells, reservoirs of water, as they from time to time shall judge necessary. [*Act of* 1859.]

Fire Districts and Departme't. (§ 187.) SEC. 7. The Common Council shall have power to organize said city into so many fire-districts as they may deem necessary, and may organize and maintain a fire department for said city, to consist of one chief engineer, two asssistant engineers, twice the number of wardens as there are wards in said city, a proper number of firemen, not exceeding fifty to each engine, such number of hook and ladder men, and such number of hose-men, as may be appointed by the said Common Council; all to have the privileges and exemptions of firemen, and to hold their appointment during the pleasure of the Common Council. [*Act of* 1859.]

Rules and Regula ions (§ 188.) SEC. 8. The Common Council may make rules and regulations for the government of the said engines, wardens, firemen, hook and ladder men, and hose-men; may prescribe their respective duties in case of fire or alarms of fire; may direct the dresses and badges of authority, to be worn by them; may prescribe and regulate the time and manner of their exercise, and may impose reasonable fines for the breach of any such regulations. [*Act of* 1859.]

Powers and duties. (§ 189.) SEC. 9. The engineers and fire-wardens, under the direction of the Common Council, shall have the custody and general superintendence of the fire-engines, engine-houses, hooks, ladders, hose, public cisterns, and other conveniences for the extinguishment and prevention of fires, and it shall be their duty to see that the same are kept in order, and to see that the laws and ordinances relative to the prevention and extinguishment of fires, are duly executed, and to make detailed and particular reports of the state of their department, and of the conduct of the firemen, hook and ladder-men, and hose-men, to the Common Council, at stated periods, to be prescribed by the Common Council, and to make such reports to the Mayor, whenever required by him; the certificate of the City Clerk that a person is or has been a fireman, shall be evidence of the facts in all courts and places, on proof of the genuineness of such certificate. [*Act of* 1859.]

(§ 190.) SEC. 10. The Common Council may, by ordinance, direct the manner in which the bells in the city shall be tolled or rung in cases of fire or alarms of fire, and may impose penalties for ringing or tolling of such bells in such manner at any other time than during a fire or alarm of fire. [*Act of* 1859.] Ringing of Bells.

(§ 191.) SEC. 11. The Common Council may provide suitable compensation for any injury that any fireman, hook and ladder man, and hose man may receive, in his person or property, in consequence of his exertions at any fire. [*Act of* 1859.] Compensation for Injuries.

(§ 192.) SEC. 12. The Common Council may, by ordinance: General Powers.

First, Prescribe the duties and powers of the engineers and wardens at fires, and in cases of alarms of fire, and may vest in them such powers as shall be deemed necessary to preserve property from being stolen, and to extinguish and prevent fires;

Second, Prescribe the powers and duties of the Mayor and Aldermen at such fires and in cases of alarm; Mayor and Aldermen.

Third, Provide for the removal and keeping away from such fires, of all idle, disorderly or suspicious persons, and may confer powers for that purpose on the engineers, fire wardens or officers of the city; Suspicious Persons.

Fourth, Provide for compelling persons to aid in the extinguishment thereof by forming lines or ranks for the purpose of carrying water, and by all proper means to aid in the preservation, removal and securing of property exposed to danger by fire; Compel aid at Fires.

Fifth, To compel the Marshal, Constables and Watchmen of Marshal and others.

the city to be present at such fires, and to perform such duties as the said Common Council shall prescribe.[a] [*Act of* 1859.]

Arrest for refusal to obey orders authorized.

(§ 193.) SEC. 13. Whenever any person shall refuse to obey any lawful order of any Engineer, Fire-Warden, Mayor or Alderman at any fire, it shall be lawful for the officer giving such order, to arrest, or to direct orally any Constable, Watchman or any citizen, to arrest such person and confine him temporarily in any safe place, until such fire shall be extinguished, and in the same manner such officers, or any of them, may arrest or direct the arrest and confinement of any person at such fire, who shall be intoxicated or disorderly. [*Act of* 1859.]

Hazardous Buildings.

(§ 194.) SEC. 14. Whenever any building in said city shall be on fire, it shall be the duty, and be lawful for the Chief Engineer, with the consent of the Mayor, or any Alderman, or for any two Aldermen, to order and direct such building, or any other building which they may deem hazardous, and likely to communicate fire to other buildings, or any part of such building, to be pulled down and destroyed, and no action shall be maintained against any person, or against the said city therefor ; but any person interested in any such building so destroyed or injured, may, within three months thereafter, apply to the Common Council to assess and pay the damages he has sustained. At the expiration of the three months, if any such application shall have been made in writing, the Common Council shall either pay the said claimant such sum as shall be agreed upon by them and the said claimant for such damages, or if no such agreement shall be effected, shall proceed to ascertain the amount of such damages, and shall provide for the appraisal, assessment, collection and payment of the same in the same manner as is provided by title seven of this act, for the ascertainment, assessment, collection and payment of damages sustained by the taking of lands for purposes of public improvement. [*Act of* 1859.]

Damages.

Provisions concerning steam crafts

(§ 195.) SEC. 15. The Common Council shall have full power and authority to prohibit by ordinance any and every steamboat, propeller, or other craft propelled or operated, either in whole or in part, by steam, from landing or approaching within one

[a] Vide. Sec. 13, Title 4.

hundred feet of any dock or wharf or bank, in said city, unless provided with a good and sufficient spark catcher, so as to prevent cinders or sparks passing into the open air, to the danger of firing any property in said city, and may enforce such ordinance by a fine not exceeding five hundred dollars against the master or owner, or person having charge of the said steamboat, propeller, or other craft, shall, by the direction or command of the master, owner, or person having charge thereof, violate the provisions of such ordinance, and be convicted thereof, and a fine being imposed therefor by the Recorder's Court, such fine and all the costs of the proceedings shall be a lien on such steamboat, propeller or other craft, and may be enforced in the name of the city against such boat, vessel, or craft, in the same manner as any other lien may be enforced. [*Act of* 1859.]

TITLE VIII.

SUPPORT OF THE POOR.

Director of the Poor, Powers of

(§ 196.) SEC. 1. The Director of the Poor elected in said city, as hereinbefore provided, shall be the Director of the Poor of said city, and shall possess all the powers and authority of Directors of the Poor of towns in this State, in relation to the support and relief of indigent persons, the binding out of children who shall solicit alms, or who, or whose parents shall become chargeable to the said city, or to the County of Saginaw, in said city; the safe keeping and care of lunatics; the care of habitual drunkards; the binding out and contracting for the service of disorderly persons; the support of bastards; and all such other powers as are conferred on Directors of the Poor in the respective towns, and shall be subject to the same duties, obligations and liabilities.[a] [*Act of* 1859.]

Indigent persons; how supported.

(§ 197.) SEC. 2. Until provisions shall otherwise be made, as hereinafter authorized, the indigent persons, and such others as shall be entitled to relief under the laws of this State, who are or shall become chargeable to the said city, being in the said city, shall continue to be supported and relieved in the manner provided by law in respect to the County of Saginaw.[b] [*Act of* 1859.]

Erection of Alms-houses authorized.

(§ 198.) SEC. 3. Whenever the Common Council shall deem it expedient, they may, by a vote of two-thirds of all the members thereof, cause an alms-house to be erected within or without the

[a] Vide, Sec. 36, Title 3.
[b] Vide, Sec. 1, Title 5.

city limits, being authorized thereto as herein provided, and may appoint as many Commissioners to take charge thereof as they may judge necessary, and may raise the expense of the maintaining of the alms-house by a tax or taxes on the real estate within the said city, and on the personal property of residents therein, in the same manner as hereinbefore provided in respect to taxes for the general expenses of the said city, and the same proceedings for that purpose shall be had in all respects.[a] [*Act of* 1859.]

(§ 199.) SEC. 4. The Common Council shall appoint such other officers and servants for the government and management of the said alms-house as they shall deem necessary, and they, together with the said Commissioners, shall hold their appointment during the pleasure of the Common Council;[b] and the Common Council shall make such regulations as they think necessary for the government, management, support and good order of the said alms-house, its tenants, officers, keepers and servants. [*Act of* 1859.] Governme't of Alms-Houses.

(§ 200.) SEC. 5. The Common Council may cause such labor in manufactures or otherwise, to be performed by the tenants of such alms-house as they shall prescribe, and may provide the materials and implements therefor at the expense of the city. [*Act of* 1859.] Labor of inmates.

(§ 201.) SEC. 6. All moneys that shall be raised in the said city by licenses to groceries, tavern-keepers or common victualers, and for penalties for the violation of any law of this State regulating the retailing of spirituous liquors, shall be paid into the city treasury, and shall belong to and constitute a part of the fund of the city for the support of the poor therein, and shall be deposited for safe keeping by the Treasurer as other moneys under his care; and accounts thereof shall be kept, and the same shall be drawn, in the manner hereinbefore prescribed in relation to the funds of said city.[c] [*Act of* 1859.] Poor Fund provided.

---

[a]Vide, Sec. 20, Title 5.
[b]Vide, Sec. 5, Title 2.
[c]Vide, Sec. 3, Title 5.

TITLE IX.

COURTS OF JUSTICE.

Recorder's Court.

(§ 202.) SEC. 1. The Recorder shall have full power and authority to hold and keep a court, which shall and is hereby declared to be a court of record, and known in the laws as and by the name of "The Recorder's Court of the City of East Saginaw," and shall have an appropriate seal, which shall be provided by the Recorder, and kept by the Clerk thereof, who shall keep a record of the proceedings of the said court. [*Act of* 1859.]

(§ 203.) SEC. 2. The Recorder may appoint a clerk of the Recorder's Court, who shall give such bonds as the Recorder shall approve, for the faithful performance of his duties, and who shall be removable at the pleasure of the Recorder. The clerk of the Recorder's Court may appoint a deputy, who shall be authorized to perform all the duties of the clerk, but the clerk and his sureties shall be reponsible for the acts of the deputy.[a] [*Act of* 1859.]

Clerk.

Deputy.

(§ 204.) SEC. 3. The jurisdiction of said Recorder's court shall extend to, and said court shall have original and exclusive jurisdiction, and shall have power to hear, try and determine all civil actions arising in said city, wherein said city, in its corporate capacity, shall be a party, or any city or ward officer, in his official character, shall be a party; all charges complaints, actions and prosecutions for the recovery of any and all forfeitures and penalties for alledged violations or infringements of the acts of the legislature of this State incorporating said city, except in cases where jurisdiction is especially given to some other court by this act; all offenses against any by-laws or ordinances of said city except as provided in section 15, of title 4, of this act as amended, and all actions for encroachments upon or injury to any of the streets, lanes, alleys, bridges, parks, or other public improvements of said city; and concurrent jurisdiction in all actions wherein the title to lands shall come in question, wherein the said city, or any city or ward officer, as such, shall be a party; and said court shall also have exclusive appellate jurisdiction of all actions brought before justices of the peace to recover forfeitures or penalties for alleged violations of any ordinances of said city, or violations of this act for the violation of which, by said ordinance or by this act, such justice of the peace has cognizance. [*Act of* 1865.]

Jurisdiction and powers of Recorder's Court.

(§ 205.) SEC. 4. Whenever either party shall demand that the cause be tried by a jury, before the trial thereof shall have been commenced, and shall pay the sum of three dollars to the clerk of said court, the Recorder shall direct the Marshal or any Constable of said city in attendance to make a list of names of twenty-four citizens, who shall be residents of said city, having the qualification of jurors in the Circuit Courts of this State, from

Trials by Jury.

How Empanneled.

[a] Vide Sec. 37, Title 4.

which list the plaintiff and defendant shall alternately strike out one until each shall have struck out six names—the person demanding the jury shall first strike out, and in case the said city shall be a party, the City Attorney shall strike on behalf of said city; if either party refuse to strike out, then the clerk shall do so in his stead, under the direction of the court; and the remaining names shall constitute the jury. When no jury is demanded, the cause shall be tried by the Recorder, unless the Recorder shall, on his own motion, order a jury, in which case a jury shall be selected as hereinbefore provided. [*Act of* 1859.]

Summons.

(§ 206.) SEC. 5. The clerk when such jury fee shall be paid shall thereupon issue a venire, directed to the Marshal or any Constable of said city, commanding such officer to summons such persons named in the venire to attend said court at a time and place therein specified to serve as jurors. [*Act of* 1859.]

Penalty for refusal to serve.

(§ 207.) SEC. 6. Every juror summoned as aforesaid, who shall neglect or refuse to attend at the time and place [named] in such venire, shall be liable to a fine of not less than one nor more than ten dollars and costs, and may be brought before the court for that purpose by attachment issued under the seal of said court tested by the [Recorder] and signed by the clerk, but no such fine shall be imposed after the period of thirty days from the time he became liable as aforesaid. [*Act of* 1859.]

Compensation.

(§ 208.) SEC. 7. Every juror serving in any cause tried in said court shall be entitled to receive the sum of twenty-five cents if the jury agree. [*Act of* 1859.]

Oath of Officer.

(§ 209.) SEC. 8. The officer shall, in all cases, before making out such list of names for jurors, be sworn to make such list without favor or partiality to either party, and in case any of the jury so summoned shall neglect or refuse to attend, or cannot be found after diligent search and inquiry in said city, or shall be excused from serving, talesmen may be summoned from the inhabitants of said city, as in other courts of record. [*Act of* 1859.]

Terms of Court.

(§ 210.) SEC. 9. The Recorder's court shall be held on the second Monday of each month, and the terms of said court may be continued until the business is disposed of; and special sessions may be held as often as may be deemed necessary for the dispatch of business, and it shall be lawful for said Recorder or Clerk to administer oaths to witnesses on the trial of a cause, to take affidavits or depositions to be read in said court under the rules and practice thereof, and to receive therefor the same fees as is allowed for similar services in the Circuit Court to the Clerk thereof. [*Act of* 1859.]

(§ 211.) SEC. 10. The Clerk of said court shall keep a journal of the proceedings of the court, under the direction of the Recorder, and all entries therein shall be read in open court by the Clerk, from day to day, and shall be corrected when necessary, and signed by the Recorder. [*Act of* 1859.] Duty of the Clerk.

(§ 212.) SEC. 11. The said journal shall be and remain a public record in the office of the clerk of said court, and shall be by him delivered over to his successor in office, together with the books and papers belonging to said office; and the Recorder's successor in office shall be authorized to continue and complete all proceedings begun by his predecessor. [*Act of* 1859.] Journal a Public Record.

(§ 213.) SEC. 12. Any record or entry made in said journal as aforesaid, may be read in evidence in all courts of justice, and in all proceedings before any officer, body or board, in which it may be necessary to refer thereto, either from the journal itself, or from a true and certified copy thereof, certified by the Clerk, with the seal of the court affixed; and in all cases whenever it shall become necessary in any action or other proceeding before said Recorder's court, to give evidence of a judgment or other proceeding had before said court, the original entry of such judgment or other proceeding shall be good evidence before said court. [*Act of* 1859.] May be read in evidence.

(§ 214.) SEC. 13. It shall be the duty of the said Clerk, either in person or by his deputy, to attend every term of said court, both general and special, and he shall have the care and custody of the seal of the said court and of the records, books and papers pertaining to the office of Clerk of said court, and filed or deposited therein. [*Act of* 1859.] Clerk to attend court.

(§ 215.) SEC. 14. The said Recorder's court shall have power to take recognizance for keeping of the peace and good behavior, and for appearance before said court, or any other court, at any day or term; and full power to punish for contempt of court by fine or imprisonment, or both, but such fine shall not exceed twenty-five dollars, nor such imprisonment sixty days. [*Act of* 1859.] Powers of Recorder's Court.

TITLE IX. COURTS OF JUSTICES

Marshal and Constables to attend. (§ 216.) SEC. 15. The Marshal, and so many Constables as may be required, shall attend the Recorder's court, and discharge all the duties of their respective offices; and the said Marshal and other ministerial officers of said city, shall execute and return all processes issuing out of said court to them directed, in the same manner as Sheriffs or other officers of courts of record in this State.[u] [*Act of* 1859.]

Rules, Executions, judgments, &c. (§ 217.) SEC. 16. The Recorder's court shall have power and authority to make all rules for the practice in such court, and may issue execution upon any judgment, fine or penalty entered by said court, and may levy and collect the amount of such judgment in the same manner as executions issued out of the Circuit Court for the County of Saginaw; such executions shall be made returnable in sixty days from the date thereof, and may authorize the taking of the body of the person against whom the execution runs; in all cases where such taking is authorized by the laws of this State on executions issuing out of the Circuit or other courts in the State, or by any ordinances of the City of East Saginaw, for the violation of which such arrest or taking is authorized. [*Act of* 1859.]

Costs and fees of officers. (§ 218.) SEC. 17. And said court shall have power, from time to time, to establish the costs and fees of all the officers of said court, which costs and fees shall not exceed those now established by the rules and practice of the Circuit Court of Saginaw County for like services, and said costs and fees shall be taken and made a part of the judgment and levied and collected therewith. The Recorder shall have the following fees:—for deciding a cause, on motion, two dollars; for trial, three dollars, which shall be in full for his services in such cause, which shall also be taxed and collected as aforesaid. [*Act of* 1859.]

Writ or process. (§ 219.) SEC. 18. All writs and process from the Recorder's court shall run in the name of the people of the State of Michigan, be directed to the Marshal or any Constable of said City, shall bear teste in the name of the Recorder, shall be sealed with the seal of said court, signed by the Clerk and dated on the day on which the same shall be issued. [*Act of* 1859.]

Actions how commenced and prosecuted. (§ 220.) SEC. 19. Actions may be commenced in said court in the same manner as is provided by law for the commencement

[u] Vide, Sec. 13, Title 4.

of suits in the Circuit Courts of this State, and to this end the City Clerk is hereby authorized to procure the necessary books, at the expense of the city, and all provisions of law relative to trials of causes in Circuit Courts shall apply to said Recorder's court, except as herein otherwise expressed, and actions for the recovery of penalties and forfeitures arising for violations of any of the ordinances or by-laws of said city of which said Recorder's court or any justice of the peace of said city has jurisdiction, may be commenced and prosecuted in the same manner as is by law provided for the recovery of fines and penalties for breach of any statute of this State; and all prosecutions for offences in said Recorder's court, arising under this act or under any ordinance or regulation of the Common Council, shall be in the name of the people of the State of Michigan, and be commenced by filing an affidavit, duly sworn to before said clerk, and subscribed by the person making the complaint, and having endorsed thereon the proper jurat of said Clerk; and it shall be deemed sufficient to set forth in said complaint the offence complained of according to its substance; the trial shall be had and determined upon said complaint and upon pleadings which may be amended in the same manner as indictments and pleadings under the general laws of this State. [*Act of* 1865.]

(§ 221.) SEC. 20. Appeals may be taken to said Recorder's court from any judgment of any Justice of the Peace elected within said city, upon any suit or prosecution for a violation of any of the provisions of this act, or of the by-laws or ordinances of said city, of which such justice has jurisdiction, by filing with the justice by whom such judgment was rendered, a like affidavit and bond or recognizance, as is or may at the time by law be required on appeals in civil cases from Justice to Circuit Courts in this State, and all such provisions of law relative to appeals from Justices Courts to the Circuit Court, shall apply, as far as practicable, to the said Recorder's Court. [*Act of* 1859.] Appeals.

(§ 222.) SEC. 21. Writs of certiorari may be sued out of said Recorder's court, to any Justice's court of said city, on any judgment rendered by such Justice of the Peace, in any action brought to recover a penalty or forfeiture for the violation of any provision of this act, or the violation of any by-laws or ordinances of said Certiorari.

city, in the same manner, as near as may be, and with the like effect as certioraris from Circuit Courts, and all provisions of law relating to certioraris from Circuit Courts in civil cases, shall apply as near as may be to the Recorder's Court, except that the allowance of such writ shall be granted by the Recorder [*Act of* 1859.]

Ibid. (§ 223.) SEC. 22. In any case of appeal from any Justice's Court within said city, or in case a certiorari shall issue from said Recorder's Court directed to such Justice, such Justice shall make a return of the proceedings had before him, in like manner in all respects, as is by law required relative to return from Justice's Courts to the Circuit Court in cases of appeal and certiorari. [*Act of* 1859.]

Ibid. (§ 224.) SEC. 23. The Recorder's Court shall have power to hear, try and determine said appeal, and the judgment of said court shall be final, except that the same may be carried to the Supreme Court, in the same manner in all respects, as cases in the Circuit Court are taken to the said Supreme Court; and said Recorder's Court shall hear and determine all matters brought before him by writ of certiorari, in the same manner as such cases are disposed of in the Circuit Court. [*Act of* 1859.]

Entry fee. (§ 225.) SEC. 24. The same entry fee shall be paid the Clerk of said court in causes commenced, or brought into the Recorder's Court, as is required in like cases in the Circuit Court, except when the cause is commenced or brought into said Recorder's Court on behalf of the city, or a city or ward officer in his official character. [*Act of* 1859.]

Removal to Supreme Court. (§ 226.) SEC. 25. Any cause commenced in the Recorder's Court, and any case brought in said court by appeal or certiorari, and determined therein, may be taken to the Supreme Court of this State, in the same manner as causes removed to said court from the Circuit Courts of this State, by bill of exception, case made, writ of error, or otherwise. [*Act of* 1859.]

Fines, penalties, &c. (§ 227.) SEC. 26. [a]It shall be the duty of the Marshal, or of any Constable, to pay into the hands of the Clerk, immediately on the receipt thereof, all fines, penalties, and costs, imposed by said Recorder's Court, who shall forthwith pay the costs to the officers

[a]Vide Sec. 3, Title 5 and Sec. 6, Title 8.

entiled thereto; and said Clerk shall, on or before the first of each month, pay such money into the city treasury, and he shall make quarterly reports to the Common Council, of all the cases disposed of in said court, stating the several entry and jury fees paid, fines and penalties imposed, the manner in which the same may have been satisfied, and the sums which he may have paid to said Treasurer from time to time, as aforesaid, which report shall be published with the proceedings of the Council. [*Act of* 1859.]

(§ 228.) SEC. 27. The said Recorder's Court shall have full power and authority to hear, try and determine, according to the laws of this State, and according to the course of common law, all offenses and misdemeanors of which said court has jurisdiction or cognizance by this act, although no by-law or ordinance shall have been made or passed relative to such offense. [*Act of* 1859.] Offences and misdemeanors.

(§ 229.) SEC. 28. Whenever any person or persons charged with any offense supposed, by such charges, to have been committed within the limits of said city, against the provisions of this act, or in violation of any by-laws or ordinances of the said city, shall depart from, lurk or reside without the limits of said city' the recorder's court in session, or the Recorder in vacation, is authorized and empowered, and it is hereby made his duty, to command the Marshal or any Constable of said city, or the Sheriff or Sheriffs of any county or counties, or any Constables of any township within this State, by a writ of capias, under the seal of said court, to arrest the body or bodies of such person or persons so charged as aforesaid, and such person or persons have before the Recorder's Court, agreeably to the exigency of said writ, to be dealt with according to law; and the officer or officers to whom such capias shall be directed and delivered are hereby required to use due dilligence in executing the same, under such pains and penalties as are by law incurred by any Sheriff or other officer neglecting or refusing to execute any capias or other process to him or them directed and delivered; and in case the person so charged as aforesaid shall be within the limits of the County of Saginaw, the writs of capias may be directed to the Marshal or any Constable of the said city, who shall be authorized to serve the same within the limits of said county; but before such capias shall issue, such person or persons preferring the charge Proceedings mentioned in this section shall file with the Clerk of the Court security for all the costs in case of acquittal, unless such charge is preferred by a public city officer; in which case no such security shall be required. [*Act of* 1859.]

City Penitentiary. (§ 230.) SEC. 29. The Common Council of said city shall have power and authority whenever they shall deem it expedient, to provide a city penitentiary, where all persons charged with, or convicted of, offences or misdemeanors against the charter, by-laws or ordinances of said city, may be confined, imprisoned, until discharged by authority of law; and the said Common Council shall appoint all officers necessary for said penitentiary, prescribe their powers and duties, regulate the time and manner such prisoners shall be kept at labor, and make all by-laws, ordinances or orders concerning the good government and regulation of said penitentiary, and for the punishment of such prisoners as may refuse to work therein, as they may deem necessary and proper. [*Act of* 1859.]

Governme't of

Who may be confined in penit ntiary. (§ 231.) SEC. 30. Any person arrested by virtue of any process issuing from any court of justice in said city, or by authority of any officer of said city, may be confined in said penitentiary, in the same manner as prisoners are or may be detained in the jail of Saginaw County; and any law of this State prohibiting escapes, aiding prisoners to escape, or any other act detrimental to the safety of prisoners in a county jail, shall apply to said prison: *Provided*, The Common Council or the Mayor or Recorder of said city may at any time direct any or all such persons to be removed from said penitentiary to the jail of the County of Saginaw: *And, provided also*, Such prisoners, or any of them, may at any time, in the first instance, be confined in the said county jail whenever the same may be deemed necessary by said Common Council; and the keeper of said jail or penitentiary shall be allowed such compensation for keeping and providing for prisoners confined therein as the Common Council may determine to be just and reasonable, not exceeding the amount allowed by the Supervisors of Saginaw County for county prisoners. [*Act of* 1859.]

Proviso.

Proviso

Use of county jail allowed. (§ 232.) SEC. 31. Until the Common Council shall have provided a city penitentiary as hereinbefore provided, the Courts of Justice in said city shall have power to imprison in the jail of the

County of Saginaw, and it is kereby made the duty of the keeper of said jail to receive such persons as are brought to his custody by authority of any of said courts, or the Common Council, or any officer of said city authorized so to commit such person, in the same manner as any court of record of this State, or other competent authority, is authorized to commit to said jail. [*Act of* 1859.]

Justices of the Peace.

(§ 233.) SEC. 32. The Justices of the Peace in the said city exercising civil jurisdiction, shall be deemed Justices of the Peace of the County of Saginaw, and shall be subject to the general laws of the State in relation to civil causes before Justices of the Peace, and appeals from their judgment may be made in the Circuit Court for the County of Saginaw, in the same manner as appeals from Justice's judgments in towns are made. [*Act of* 1859.]

Ibid.

(§ 234.) SEC. 33. The Justices of the Peace of said city shall have all the authority of Justices of the Peace in towns in criminal matters, and shall have all the authority and perform all the duties hereinbefore provided and required of them, and shall hold, a session of court daily, if necessary. [*Act of* 1859.]

Certain Suits, how brought.

(§ 235.) SEC. 34. All suits which shall be brought to recover any penalty or forfeiture for the violation of any ordinance of the Common Council, shall be brought in the name of the City of East Saginaw, under the direction of the Common Council, or of the Attorney of said city, and no person being an inhabitant, freeman or freeholder of the said city, shall be disqualified for that cause from acting as a judge, justice or juror in the trial or other proceeding, in any suit, brought to recover a forfeiture or penalty for the violation of any provisions of this act, or for the violation of any ordinance of the Common Council, nor from serving any process summoning a jury in such suit, or from acting in any such capacity, or being a witness on the trial of any issue, or upon the taking or making any inquisition or assessment, or any judicial investigation of facts, to which issue, inquest or investigation the said city, or any city or ward officer, is a party, or in which said city or such officer is interested; nor shall any judge of any court be disqualified to hear and adjudicate on an appeal in any matter originating in said city, because he is an inhabitant thereof. [*Act of* 1859.]

Citizens not disqualified.

TITLE IX. COURTS OF JUSTICE.

Judgments against the city may be appealed.

(§ 236.) SEC. 35. If any judgment in any action shall be rendered against the city by any Justice of the Peace, such judgment may be removed by appeal to the Recorder's Court of the (city) of East Saginaw, in the same manner and with the same effect as though the city were a natural person, except that no bond or recognizence, to the adverse-party, shall be necessary to be executed by or on behalf of said city. [*Act of* 1859.]

Execution to issue immediately.

(§ 237.) SEC. 36. Every execution for any penalty or forfeiture recovered for the violation of any of the provisions of this act, or for the violation of any by-laws or ordinance of said city, may be issued immediately on the rendition of the judgment, and shall command the amount to be made of the property of the defendant, if any such can be found, and if not, then to commit the defendant to the county jail or city penitentiary, for such time as shall have been directed by the ordinance of the Common Council or the judgment of the court. [*Act of* 1859.]

Moneys, how applied

(§ 238.) SEC. 37. The Common Council may direct any moneys that may have been recovered for penalties or forfeitures to be applied to the payment of any extra expenses that may have been incurred in apprehending offenders or in subpœnaing or defraying the expenses of witnesses in any suit for such penalties or forfeitures, or in conducting such suits. [*Act of* 1859.]

Who to be deemed Vagrants.

How punished.

(§ 239.) SEC. 38. All persons being habitual drunkards, destitute and without visible means of support, or who being such habitual drunkards, shall abandon, neglect or refuse to aid in the support of their families, being complained of by such families; all able-bodied and sturdy beggars who may apply for alms or solicit charity; all persons wandering abroad, lodging in watch-houses, out houses, market places, sheds, stables, or uninhabited dwellings, or in the open air, and not giving a good account of themselves; all common brawlers and disturbers of the public quiet; all persons wandering abroad and begging, or who go about from door to door, or place themselves in streets, highways, passages or other public places, or beg or receive alms within the said city, shall be deemed vagrants, and may upon conviction before any Justice of the Peace in said city, be sentenced to confinement at hard labor in the county jail or city penitentiary for any time not exceeding sixty days. [*Act of* 1859.]

(§ 240.) SEC. 39. All persons who shall have actually abandoned their wives or children in the City of East Saginaw, or who may neglect to provide according to their means for their wives or children, are hereby declared to be disorderly persons within the meaning of chapter thirty-nine of title nine of the revised statutes of eighteen hundred and forty-six, and may be proceeded against as such, in the manner directed by said title; and it shall be the duty of the magistrate before whom any such person may be brought for examination, to judge and determine from the facts and circumstances of the case whether the conduct of such person amounts to such deseation or neglect to provide for his wife or children. [*Act of* 1859.]

Disorderly Persons.

How punished.

TITLE X.*

PUBLIC HEALTH.

Board of Health.

(§ 241.) SEC. 1. The Common Council of said city may constitute a Board of Health for said city, and may appoint a competent physician to be the health officer thereof.

Powers and duties.

(§ 242.) SEC. 2. The said Board of Health shall have power, and it shall be their duty, to take such measures as they shall deem effectual to prevent the entrance of any pestilential or infectious disease into the city; to stop, detain, and examine, for that purpose, every person coming from any place infected, or believed to be infected, with such a disease; to establish, maintain and regulate a pest-house or hospital, at some place within the city, or not exceeding three miles beyond its bounds; to cause any person not being a resident of the city, or if a resident of the city, who is not an inhabitant of this State, and who shall be, or be suspected of being, infected with any such disease, to be sent to such pest-house or hospital; to cause any resident of the city infected with any such disease, to be removed to such pest-house or hospital, if the health physician and two other physicians of the city, including the attending physician of the sick person, if he have one, shall certify that the removal of such resident is necessary for the preservation of the public health; to remove from the city or destroy any furniture, wearing-apparel, or goods, wares or merchan-

Pest House Hospital.

Inspected Goods.

*[Act of 1859.]

dise, or other articles or property of any kind, which shall be suspected of being tainted or infected with any pestilence, or which shall be, or be likely to pass into such a state as to generate and propagate disease; to abate all nuisances of every description, which are or may be injurious to the public health, in any way and in any manner they may deem expedient; and from time to time to do all acts, make all regulations, and pass all ordinances which they shall deem necessary or expedient for the preservation of health and suppression of disease in the city, and to carry into effect and execute the powers hereby granted.

(§ 243.) SEC. 3. The captain, master, or person in charge of any steamboat or other craft or vessel which shall enter the city, having on board thereof any person sick of any malignant fever or other pestilential or infectious disease, shall be guilty of a misdemeanor, punishable by fine or imprisonment, unless the person so diseased, became so on the way, and could not be left. It shall be the duty of such captain, master, or person in charge, within two hours after his arrival, to report in writing to the Mayor, or some health officer, the fact of such sick person's being on board, and the name, description and location of his craft; and he shall not permit such sick person to land or to be landed, until the board of health, or some member thereof, shall give permission for that purpose; and any neglect or violation of these provisions, or of any or either of them, shall be a misdemeanor, punishable with fine and imprisonment.

Duties of Captains of Vessels, &c.

Penalty.

(§ 244.) SEC. 4. The owner, driver, conductor, or person in charge of any stage-coach, railroad car, or other public conveyance which shall enter the city, having on board any person sick of a malignant fever or pestilential or infectious disease, shall, within two hours after the arrival of such sick person, report in writing the fact, with the name of such person, and the house or place where he was put down in the city, to the Mayor, or some member or officer of the Board of Health; and any and every neglect to comply with these provisions or any of them, shall be a misdemeanor, punishable with fine and imprisonment.

Conductors of Public conveyance, to report.

Penalty.

(§ 245.) SEC. 5. Any person who shall, knowingly, bring or procure, or cause to be brought into the city any property of any kind, tainted or infected with any malignant fever or pestilential or infectious disease, shall be guilty of misdemeanor, punishable by fine and imprisonment.

Quarentine for Steamboats and Vessels.

(§ 246.) SEC. 6. The Board of Health shall have power, by an order in writing for that purpose, to be served on the captain, master, or person in charge of any steamboat or other vessel or craft, or any owner or consignee thereof, if such boat, craft or vessel be by them suspected to have on board any infected or diseased person or property, to require such boat or vessel not to enter the city, or to remove to some certain distance, not exceeding three miles from the city; and every such captain, master, person in charge, consignee or owner, who shall be served with such order, shall be guilty of a misdemeanor, punishable with fine and imprisonment, if such boat, vessel or craft shall enter the city in violation of such order, or shall not be removed according to the tenor of such order, within a reasonable time, not exceeding three hours after the service of such notice.

Penalty.

Inn-keepers to report.

(§ 247.) SEC. 7. Every keeper of an inn or boarding-house or lodging-house in the city, who shall have in his house at any time any sick traveler, boatman or sailor, shall report the fact, and the name of the person, in writing, within six hours after he came to the house or was taken sick therein, to the Mayor, or some officer or member of the Board of Health; every physician in the city shall report under his hand to one of the officers above named, the name residence and disease of every patient he shall have, sick of any infectious or pestilential disease, within six hours after he shall have visited such patient. A violation of either of the provisions of this section, or of any part of either of them, shall be a misdemeanor, punishable by fine and imprisonment; the fine not to exceed one hundred dollars, nor the imprisonment six months.

Physicians to report.

Penalty.

Moneys for Fines, how applied.

(§ 248.) SEC. 8. All fines imposed under the last five sections shall belong to the city, and when collected shall be paid into the City Treasury, and be devoted to the maintenance and support of the pest-house or of any hospital that may hereafter be established by the city.

General Powers of Common Council to preserve health, cleanliness of city, &c.

(§ 249.) SEC. 9. The Common Council shall have power to pass and enact such by-laws and ordinances as they from time to time shall deem necessary and proper, for the filling up, draining, cleansing, cleaning and regulating any grounds, yards, basins, slips or cellars, within the said city, that shall be sunken, damp, foul, incumbered with filth, and rubbish, or unwholesome, and for filing or altering and amending all sinks and privies within the said city, and for directing the mode of constructing them in future, and to cause all such work as may be necessary for the purpose aforesaid, and for the preservation of the public health and the cleanliness of the city, to be executed and done at the expense of the city corporation, on account of the persons respectively upon whom the same may be assessed, and for that purpose to cause the expenses thereof to be estimated, assessed and collected, and the lands charged therewith to be sold in case of non-payment, in the same manner as is provided by law with respect to other public improvements within said city; and in all cases where the said by-laws or ordinances shall require anything to be done in respect to the property of several persons, the expenses thereof may be included in one assessment, and the several houses and lots in respect to which such expenses shall have been incurred, shall be briefly described in the manner required by law in the assessment roll for the general expenses of the city, and the sum of money assessed to each owner or occupant of any such house or lot shall be the amount of money expended in making such improvement upon such premises, together with a rateable proportion of the expenses of assessing and collecting the moneys expended in making such improvements.

Expenses; how defrayed.

(§ 250.) SEC. 10. Whenever, in the opinion of the Common Council, any building, fence, or other erection of any kind, or any part thereof, is liable to fall down, and persons or property may thereby be endangered, they may order any owner or occupant of the premises on which such building, fence, or other erection stands, to take down the same, or any part thereof, within a reasonable time, to be fixed by the order, or immediately, as the case may require, or in case the order is not complied with, cause the same to be taken down at the expense of the city, on account of the owner of the premises, and assess the expense on the land on which it stood. The order, if not immediate in its terms, may be served on any occupant of the premises, or be published in the city paper, as the Common Council shall direct.

Unsafe buildings, fences, &c.

Expenses, how defrayed.

TITLE X. PUBLIC HEALTH.

Duty of City Clerk.

(§ 251.) SEC. 11. The City Clerk shall be Clerk of the said Board of Health, and it shall be his duty to attend the meetings thereof, and to keep a record of its proceedings, and such record, or a duly certified copy of the same, or of any part thereof, shall be *prima facie* evidence of the facts therein contained in any court, or before any officer.

TITLE XI.

MISCELLANEOUS PROVISIONS.

(§ 252.) SEC. 1. The Common Council, or the Mayor or other officer whose duty it shall be to judge of the sufficiency of the proposed sureties of any officer of whom a bond or instrument in writing may be required under the provisions of this act, shall examine into the sufficiency of such sureties, and shall require them to submit to an examination under oath as to their property; such oath may be administered by the Mayor or any Alderman of said city. The deposition of the surety shall be reduced to writing be signed by him, certified by the person taking the same, and annexed to and filed with the bond or instrument in writing to which it relates. [*Act of* 1859.] **Sureties.** **Examine on Oath.**

(§ 253.) SEC. 2. The Mayor or Chairman of any committee or special committee of the Common Council, shall have power to administer any oath or take any affidavit in respect to any matter **Ibid.**

pending before the Common Council or such committee.[a] [*Act of* 1859.]

Perjury. (§ 254. SEC. 3. Any person who may be required to take any oath or affirmation under or by virtue of any provisions of this act, who shall, under such oath or affirmation, in any statement or affidavit or otherwise, wilfully swear falsely as to any material fact or matter, shall be guilty of perjury. [*Act of* 1859.]

Costs in suits against officers. (§ 255.) SEC. 4. If any suit shall be commenced against any person elected or appointed under this act to any office, for any act done or omitted to be done under such election or appointment or against any person having done any thing, or act by the command of any such officer, and if final judgment be rendered in such suit whereby any such defendant shall be entitled to costs. he shall recover double costs in the manner defined by law. [*Act of* 1859.]

Acts repealed. (§ 256.) SEC. 5. All former acts and parts of acts relating to the Village of East Saginaw, not expressly embodied in or made a

Rights not affected. part of this act, are hereby repealed; but nothing herein contained shall be construed to destroy, impair or take away any right or remedy acquired or given by any act hereby repealed and all proceedings commenced under any such former act shall be carried out and completed, and all prosecutions for any offense committed, or penalty or forfeiture incurred, shall be enforced in the same manner in all respects, and with the same effect, as if this act had not been passed; but nothing in this section contained shall be so construed as to annul, or impair or affect any ordinance, by-law or resolution of said Village, not inconsistent with the provisions of this act, but the same shall conttnue and be in full force until the same are amended or repealed, as fully as though this act had not been enacted. [*Act of* 1859.]

Village Officers. (§ 257.) SEC. 6. All the officers of the Village of East Saginaw, shall continue in office until the first Monday in March, A. D. one thousand eight hundred and fifty-nine, and until their successors shall be elected under this act and qualified. The present Common Council of the said village shall appoint and give notice of the place in each ward for holding the first charter election under this act, in the same title (time) and manner required

[a] Vide Sec. 37, Title 3.

of the Common Council by title two of this act; and at such first election the electors present in each ward shall choose viva voce, three Inspectors of election, who for the receiving, canvas and return of votes, and all other matters relating to said first election, shall possess all the powers of Inspectors of election under this act, and shall each take an oath of office, before any person authorized to administer oaths, before opening the polls. They shall then appoint the Clerks of the election, and proceed in all things as Inspectors of election are required to proceed under this act. It is hereby made the duty of the present Common Council to provide two ballot boxes for each ward in said city, one for ward ballots and one for city ballots. [*Act of* 1859.]

(§ 258.) Sec. 7. The present Common Council shall be and they are hereby constituted the Common Council of the City of East Saginaw, and to continue and act as such until a Common Council shall be elected and qualified under this act; and shall, while they constitute the Common Council of said city, perform all the duties and possess all the powers by this act conferred on the Common Council of the city. [*Act of* 1859.] Ibid.

(§ 259.) SEC. 8. This act shall be deemed a public act, and favorably construed, and the legislature may at any time repeal, modify or alter the same. [*Act of* 1859.] A Public Act.

(§ 260.) SEC. 9. The Recorder's Court shall possess all the power of Courts of common law and Courts of Record in this State, to carry into effect the jurisdiction and powers conferred upon it by this act. [*Act of* 1859.] Recorder's Court.

(§ 261.) SEC. 10. All process issued against said city shall run against said city in the corporate name thereof, and such process shall be served by leaving a true and attested copy of such process with the Mayor or Clerk of said city, at least ten days before the day of appearance mentioned therein. [*Act of* 1859.] Process against city, how served.

(§ 262.) SEC. 11. The corporation created by this act shall pay and discharge all the debts, obligations, contracts and liabilities of the Common Council of the Village of East Saginaw and suits may be brcught and prosecuted thereon in the same manner either in law or equity and with the same effect as they could be brought or prosecuted against the Common Cauncil of the Village of East Saginaw, if this act had not passed. [*Act of* 1859.] City liable for debts.

TITLE XI. MISCELLANEOUS PROVISIONS.

Property of Village to vest in city. (§ 263.) SEC. 12. All property, real, personal and mixed, and rights of property, in law or in equity, and all debts, fines, penalties, forfeitures, rights and causes of action, and all rights and powers not inconsistent with the provisions of this act, which belong, have accrued or may accrue, to the Common Council of the Village of East Saginaw, or to the inhabitants of the said village in their corporate capacity, shall be and the same are hereby declared to be fully and absolutely vested in the corporation created by this act, to be held subject to the provisions hereof and may be prosecuted for and recovered or claimed, asserted and maintained, by said corporation in its own name, or in any other lawful manner. [*Act of* 1859.]

Ordinances to remain in force. (§ 264.) SEC. 13. All ordinances, by-laws, regulations, resolutions and rules of the Cummon Council of the Village of East Saginaw, now in force, and not inconsistent with this act, shall remain in force until altered, amended or repealed by the Common Council, under this act, and after the same shall take effect. [*Act of* 1859.]

Proofs of Publication. (§ 265.) SEC. 14. Proof of the requisite publication of any ordinance, resolution or other proceeding required to be published in any newspaper, by the affidavit of a printer or publisher thereof taken before any officer authorized to administer oaths and take affidavits, and duly filed with the Clerk of the city or any other competent proof shall in all courts and places be conclusive evidence of the legal publication of such ordinance, resolution or other proceeding. [*Act of* 1859.]

Unpaid Taxes to continue a lien. (§ 266.) SEC. 15. All taxes and assessments returned unpaid in the Village of East Saginaw, at the time this act takes effect as law, shall continue to be a lien on the land on which the same were assessed, and shall, with the interest thereon at the rate of twenty per cent. per annum, from the time they were returned; be re-assessed by the Controller on the same property returned, and such lands shall be sold for the said taxes in the same manner and with the same effect as for ordinary city taxes. [*Act of* 1859.]

Estimate for assessment. (§ 267.) SEC. 16. For the purpose of ascertaining the sum to raised the first year under this charter, the assessment roll of the Village of East Saginaw for the year one thousand eight hundred and fifty-eight, shall be taken and deemed to be the assessment roll of the preceding year, as mentioned in title five, section two, of this act. [*Act of* 1859.]

(§ 268.) SEC. 17. The dockets, and all the books of the present Justices of the Peace residing in the territory hereby incorporated, shall be by them delivered to the Clerk of the city, as soon as he is qualified under this act, and by him delivered to some one or more of the Justices elected under this act, within six days after they shall be qualified, and thereupon such Clerk shall give notice of the dockets, books and papers delivered, and the name of the Justice to whom they are so delivered, for two weeks, by publishing the same in a newspaper published in said city, and all suits and matters pending and undetermined before any such Justice, shall be continued, and may be heard, tried and determined before the Justice to whom such dockets, books and papers shall be delivered: *Provided*, That the parties to every such suit or matter their agents or attorneys, shall be notified by such Justice at least six days before any such cause shall be tried, and the Justice or Justices of said city, to whom any such dockets, books and papers may be delivered by said Clerk, may proceed to issue execution on any jndgment thereon, and do and perform any and all acts and things touching the same that might have been done by the Justice in whose possession such dockets, books and papers now are. [*Act of* 1859.]

Books, Dockets, &c.

Pending suits.

(§ 269.) SEC. 18. This act is ordered to take effect on the twenty-eighth day of February, A. D. one thousand eight hundred and fifty-nine. [*Act of* 1859.]

Take effect.

(§ 270.) SEC. 19. The act entitled "an act to amend an act to incorporate the Village of East Saginaw, approved February thirteenth, one thousand eight hundred and fifty-five," approved February twelfth, one thousand eight hundred and fifty-seven, is hereby repealed. [*Act of* 1859.]

Repealed.

(§ 271.) SEC. 20. That whenever any additions to said city or subdivisions of any blocks or parts thereof within the limits thereof shall be hereafter laid out, the proprietors of such addition or subdivision shall, besides complying with the requirements of the laws of this State, in relation thereto, before the same shall become operative or be entitled to record, file a copy thereof with the

Plats and Additions to be submitted to Council for approval.

comptroller, and submit the same to the Common Council of said city for their approval or rejection, and if not approved, the same shall not be recorded nor become a plat; and any person who shall violate the provisions of this section shall, on conviction, be fined the sum of five hundred dollars, or imprisonment ninety days, or both, in the discretion of the court; and any person who shall sell any lot or lots by reference to any such rejected addition or subdivision shall, on conviction, be fined one hundred dollars for each lot so sold, or imprisoned thirty days, or both, in the discretion of the court. [*Act of* 1867.]

Penalty.

Title of Ordinances. (§ 272.) SEC. 21. The style of all ordinances of said city shall be as follows: "Be it ordained by the Common Council of the City of East Saginaw, as follows:" [*Act of* 1869.]

Rights to Petition. (§ 273.) SEC. 22. The inhabitants of said city shall at all times have the right to petition the Common Council. [*Act of* 1869.]

Special Franchise. (§ 274.) SEC. 23. The Common Council shall not grant any special franchise for a longer term than thirty years, nor grant exclusive privileges to the use of the streets or public grounds of said city. And the Common Council shall have power to prescribe rates of specific taxation for all franchises or privileges granted by said Council, and the manner of collection of such specific taxes. [*Act of* 1869.]

May be taxed.

Remit taxes in certain cases. (§ 275.) SEC. 24. The Common Council shall have power, whenever it shall appear that any taxes or assessments have been improperly or illegally made, assessed or collected, by a two-thirds vote of all the members elected, to cause such assessment or tax to be remitted or refunded; but no such action on the part of the Council shall in any way affect or invalidate any other tax or assessment assessed, levied or collected in said city. [*Act of* 1869.]

Fiscal year. (§ 276.) SEC. 25. The fiscal year of said city shall commence on the first day of March in each year, and all annual reports required by this act to be made, shall include all transactions of said city up to and including the last day of February preceeding. [*Act of* 1869.]

Council to publish Ordinances, &c (§ 277.) SEC. 26. The Common Council of said city shall, during the year 1869, and as often thereafter as they shall deem expedient, cause all the acts and parts of acts of incorporation of said city that may be in force, including such general laws as they may deem necessary for the use of the Mayor, Aldermen or other officers thereof, as may be necessary to the proper understanding of their duties, together with all ordinances of said city, revised and corrected so as to conform to the provisions of said acts, and properly arranged and indexed, to be published in book form, and properly certified to by the clerk thereof, and when so compiled and published, the same shall be considered the official copy of all said acts and ordinances as contemplated in the second paragraph of section fourteen, of title three of this act. Each officer of said city shall be entitled to the use of a copy by virtue of his office, and the Council may authorize the sale of copies thereof to re-imburse the city for the expense of compiling and publishing of the same. [*Act of* 1869.]

(§ 278.) SEC. 27. The Common Council, as now constituted, shall continue to exercise all the powers and duties of the Common Council of said city, as herein authorized, until the next annual election, and the organization of the new Council then elected, and the present Council shall be authorized, and it shall be its duty to designate places of election in the wards hereby constituted, and appoint inspectors of said election whenever there shall be vacancies in the board, and take all other necessary steps for carrying into effect the provisions of this amendatory act. [*Act of* 1869.] **Duties of old Council.**

(§ 279.) SEC. 28. The Board of Registration of said city, as now constituted, shall meet at the Common Council room in said city, on the third Tuesday in March next, at 10 o'clock A. M., and shall organize as provided in the "act further to preserve the purity of elections and guard against the abuses of the elective franchise by a registration of electors, approved Feb. 14, 1859," and shall, as therein provided, procure new books for registration in all the wards of said city, and take all the steps necessary for a new registration, by wards, as herein described and set off, of all the electors of said city; for this purpose said board shall proceed to apportion their members among the several wards, and in such wards as there shall be vacancies in the office of Aldermen, said board shall designate some Justice of the Peace, or some competent citizen thereof, to perform the duties of register, and such appointment shall be deemed legal and valid, and vest such person appointed with all **Registrati'n of Electors.**

the rights, privileges, powers, duties and penalties of a member of said board, as provided and prescribed in said act. For the purposes of such new registration, the said board shall cause public notice to be given, that the several ward registers will meet at some place to be designated in said notice, on the last Thursday, Friday and Saturday in March, 1869, (being the 25th, 26th and 27th days of said month of March, 1869,) and continue in session from nine o'clock in the forenoon until twelve o'clock, noon, and from two o'clock until eight o'clock in the afternoon of each of said days; and during such session, such registers shall register, or cause to be registered, all qualified electors in the several wards as provided in said act for the first registration in cities, and no others; and the proceedings of said Boards of Registration shall conform in all respects to the provisions of said act, and the registration so made shall be held and deemed a legal registration, within the meaning and terms of said act for the several wards of said city of East Saginaw, and thereafter all registrations in said city and wards shall be conducted as in said act provided and directed. No person, whose name does not appear in said registers at the annual election next ensuing, shall be entitled or allowed to vote, except in such cases and in the manner excepted and provided by said act. Any Alderman, Justice of the Peace, or other person appointed to act under this section, who shall neglect or refuse to perform the duties required in this section or by said act, shall be deemed guilty of and may be punished as for a misdemeanor, and such registration shall not be vitiated or fail by reason of such refusal or neglect, but any other member of said board may perform said duties, and their acts shall be deemed regular and lawful for all the purposes of such registration. [*Act of* 1869.]

TITLE XII.

SEWERS—BOARD OF SEWER COMMISSIONERS; CONSTRUCTION; MAINTAINANCE; ASSESSMENTS.

(§ 280.) SEC. 1. There shall be appointed by the Common Council at their first regular meeting in the month of April, 1867, three Sewer Commissioners, who shall hold their office for the terms of one, two and three years respectively, and the term for which each one is appointed shall be designated in the resolution of appointment, and in the month of April each year thereafter, there shall be appointed one Sewer Commissioner, to hold his office for three years, who shall qualify as in the charter prescribed. [*Act of* 1867.] Board of Sewer Commissioners.

(§ 281.) SEC. 2. The said Sewer Commissioners shall, as soon after their appointment in each year as practicable, organize as a Sewer Board, by the election of one of its own members president, and one of its own members acting Sewer Commissioner, and shall Organizati'n appoint, subject to the approval of the Common Council, a Sewer Engineer, who shall act as Secretary of the Board and keep the records, plans and papers of the Board, and the same are hereby declared public records. The salary or pay of the Commissioners and Sewer Engineer shall be such as the Common Council shall by resolution determine. [*Act of* 1867.]

Engineer.

Compensation.

Duties of Commiss'rs.

(§ 282.) SEC. 3. The said Sewer Commissioners shall have exclusive superintendence and management of all sewers, drains or pools now constructed, or to be constructed, and shall make all rules and regulations relative to the use and preservation of sewers and all private drains entering sewers. [*Act of* 1867.]

Expenses and Assessments.

(§ 283. SEC. 4. The current cost of altering, repairing and cleaning sewers and drains, and all incidental expenses of management, shall be estimated by the Sewer Board, who shall report the same to the Common Council on or before the last Saturday in May in each year, the amount so estimated and required for the next ensuing year, and when the same is approved by the Common Council, shall be assessed by the Assessor upon the real and personal property in the city of East Saginaw, and included in the next annual tax and tax-roll of said city, placed in the sewer tax column, and when collected, placed to the credit of the sewer fund. [*Act of* 1869.]

Plan of Sewerage.

(§ 284.) SEC. 5. The said Sewer Commissioners shall have power to devise and frame a plan of drainage and sewerage of the whole of said city upon a regular system, for the purpose of thoroughly draining and carrying off the water and filth proper to be carried off by sewers, for the health and convenience of the inhabitants of said city The plan shall show the location, direction and size of each drain and sewer, whether mains or laterals, and connections with other drains and sewers, and such other particulars as may be necessary and proper for the purpose of presenting a complete and entire plan of such drainage and sewerage. [*Act of* 1867.]

Notice and approval of plan.

(§ 285.) SEC. 6. Whenever the said Commissioner shall have prepared the said plan of drainage and sewerage, in whole or in part, of said city, they shall cause public notice to be given in all the newspapers in the city of East Saginaw, that such plan has been filed in their office for inspection, and that they will meet at a time and place in said city, to be specified in said notice, not less than ten days after the first publication of such notice, when and where they will receive the views and suggestions and objections of any parties interested in the drainage and sewerage of said city. The said Commissioners shall hear such parties at the time and place so specified, or at any adjourned meeting then and there proclaimed and shall thereupon amend and correct the same as they may deem proper, and when the said plan is so prepared and corrected, the same shall be submitted to the Common Council, and upon its being adopted and confirmed by that body, and certified to by the City Clerk and said Board of Sewer Commissioners, shall be filed in the office of the Register of Deeds of Saginaw County, whereupon the plan or any part thereof, therein set forth, shall become the permanent plan of sewerage of said city, subject to be changed only by the unanimous recommendation of said Board, and of the votes of two-thirds of the members of the Common Council, certified and filed as herein provided. [*Act of* 1867.]

Confirmed by Council. Recorded. How chag'd

(§ 286.) SEC. 7. The said Board shall, upon filing said plan, recommend to the Common Council the building of such sewers and drains as should be constructed in that year, and shall, in the month of April in each year thereafter, report to the Common Council what public sewers or drains they deem necessary to build in that year, and shall accompany the report with an estimate of the cost of each and all such drains and sewers. [*Act of* 1867.]

Board to recomend Sewers to be built, &c.

(§ 287.) SEC. 8. The Common Council shall decide what public sewers and drains of those recommended by the Sewer Board, or otherwise, in accordance with such sewerage plan, shall be built and shall through the City Clerk, notify the Board of their decision; and said Board shall proceed to advertise for proposals to build the sewers and drains ordered to be built by the Common Council, under such specifications and forms as said Board shall deem necessary, which advertisement shall be published at least fifteen days in the newspaper contracted with to do the city printing, and shall state the time and place, where and when such proposals shall be received, and the work so advertised shall be awarded to the lowest bidder, who will give good and sufficient

How Sewers shall be built. Board to advertise for Proposals. Work to be awarded to lowest bidder.

security, as required by said Board, for the furnishing of sufficient and suitable material therefor, and the prompt and faithful execution of such work. But said Board shall have the right to reject all bids, and shall in no case proceed with the construction of any sewer, except upon advertisement for proposals for the construction of the same, as herein provided. When said Board shall have made such award, they shall furnish the City Attorney with the necessary plans and specifications of the work so awarded, and he shall draw the necessary contract for the work in accordance therewith; and when approved by them, shall be executed on the part of the city by said Board, and attested by the City Clerk, under the corporate seal of the city, and shall, when executed, be in the keeping of said Board, whose duty it shall be to see that the contractor performs the same. [*Act of* 1867.]

Right to reject Proposals.

City Attorney to draw contract.

Attested. Filed.

Board to certify all expenses.

(§ 288.) SEC. 9. Said Board shall certify to the amount due upon all contracts and for all materials furnished and labor performed in building or repairing sewers, drains or pools, and all bills and accounts thus certified for amounts so due, shall be audited by the Controller, and presented by him to the Common Council in the same manner as other bills and accounts against said city. [*Act of* 1867.]

Controller to Audit same.

Limitation of Power of Board.

(§ 289.) SEC. 10. Said Board shall not lay down or construct any sewer or drain in said city, or purchase any material, or enter into any contract, except as herein provided, and except in case of any unexpected casualty or damage to the sewers or drains of said city, in which case said Board may cause the same to be repaired to an amount not exceeding five hundred dollars: *Provided, however*, That if, in any case, after advertising as above, no proposals shall be received or approved, as provided in this act, said Commissioners may build any sewer, enter into contracts, and procure material therefor, as said Commissioners may deem expedient, subject to the approval of the Common Council first obtained. [*Act of* 1867.]

Proviso.

Common Council may issue Bonds.

(§ 290.) SEC. 11. To meet the cash outlay in the construction of sewers, in anticipation of the collection of assessments and taxes therefor, as the Common Council may by resolution deem necessary, the Mayor, Controller and Clerk of said city shall, from time to time, as so required, borrow such sums not to exceed seventy-five thousand dollars outstanding, at any one time, upon the bonds of said city, which they are hereby authorized to issue for that purpose, bearing interest not to exceed ten per cent. per annum, and payable in four, seven and ten years from their respective dates, said bonds to be endorsed "sewer bonds," and to be numbered consecutively; said bonds shall not be sold for less than par, and the proceeds of the same shall be paid to the City Treasurer, and by him placed to the credit of the sewer fund. [*Act of* 1867.]

(§ 291.) SEC. 12. The assessment for the cost of the construction of lateral sewers shall be made by three (3) Commissioners, appointed by the Common Council, of whom the acting Sewer Commissioner shall be one member; or the Board of Sewer Commissioners may be appointed the assessing commissioners. [*Act of* 1867.] **Assessment of cost of lateral Sewers.**

(§ 292.) SEC. 13. The expense attending the construction of sewers shall be borne as follows, that is to say: The amount of so much of the expense of constructing any main drain or sewer as shall, in the opinion of the Sewer Commissioners, exceed the cost of a proper lateral drain or sewer for the street in which such main drain or sewer shall be laid, shall be certified to the Assessor by the Board of Sewer Commissioners, and shall be assessed upon the owners of lands and personal property included within the corporate limits of the City of East Saginaw, in proportion to the assessed valuation of the property in said city. The balance of such expenses for the construction of any main drain or sewer, and the expenses of constructing any lateral drain or sewer, shall be assessed by the said assessing Commissioners upon the lots deemed to be benefited thereby, through or near which such drain or sewer shall be laid, in proportion to the benefit derived by them respectively. [*Act of* 1869.] **Expense of construction How asses'd**

(§ 293.) SEC. 14. The said assessing Commissioners shall cause assessments for the expenses aforesaid of each lateral sewer constructed, to be made out in proper form, with diagrams showing the property assessed, and the names of the owners thereof, when known; and when such assessment is made, the said Com- **Lateral Sewers, how assessed.**

missioners shall submit the same to the Common Council. [*Act of* 1867.]

Notice to parties assessed.

(§ 294) SEC. 15. Upon such submission as aforesaid, the Clerk of the city shall cause notices of the same, with the names of all parties interested, to be published in the city newspaper for at least two weeks, and that the Common Council will, on such day as they shall appoint, proceed to hear any appeals from the said assessment. [*Act of* 1867.]

Confirmat'n of assesm't.

(§ 2 5) SEC. 16. At the day of hearing, the Common Council shall proceed in relation thereto as provided in section 43, title 6, of this act. [*Act of* 1867.]

Manner of assessing and collecting Sewer taxes.

(§ 296.) SEC. 17. When any assessment for the construction of sewers shall have been confirmed by the Common Council, the said assessment roll shall be attested by the City Clerk, under seal, and it shall be deposited with the City Assessor, who shall be responsible for its safe keeping for the purposes herein specified. The said assessor shall divide the same into nine equal parts, one of which shall be placed upon and form part of the annual taxes of said city in each year thereafter, until the same is all assessed upon said annual tax rolls, and paid. And in addition to the one-ninth of the said assessments and one-ninth of all bonds and other sewer construction expenses, otherwise unprovided for, the said assessor shall add to and include in the annual tax roll, in the sewer column thereof, the interest falling due upon all the sewer bonds in each year, and all other assessments and amounts certified to him by the Common Council, the Board of Sewer Commissioners, and also the estimated amounts for annual repairs, as hereinbefore provided for, and all such sewer taxes, when so assessed by the Assessor, shall become a lien upon the premises assessed, the same as other city taxes, and so remain, until paid; and the payment thereof shall be enforced and collected in the same manner as the general taxes of said city; and for non-payment thereof, the premises may be sold in the same manner as for non-payment of other taxes levied in said city; and when so collected shall be placed to the credit of the sewer fund, and shall be applied to the payment of the interest on said sewer bonds, and of the principal of said bonds, as they shall fall due, and for repairs, and for no other purposes. [*Act of* 1869.]

(§ 297.) SEC. 18. After payment into the treasury of any money received for assessments or taxes under the sewerage system, the City Treasurer may, under the direction of the Finance Committee of the Common Council, invest such sums not required to pay expenditures, interest or bonds during the current year, in stocks of the United States or of this State, or purchase therewith unmatured sewer bonds of said city, as may be most expedient or beneficial to the city. [*Act of* 1867.] Funds may be invested.

(§ 298.) SEC. 19. In case said Commissioners shall, in devising and framing a plan of sewerage and drainage, find it necessary to construct a sewer through any part of any street, or other property not opened by law, and such sewer or drain cannot be constructed so as to properly drain any portion of said city, without carrying the same through any part of said street or other property not opened as public, it shall be lawful for said Commissioners, or a majority of them, to present a petition to the Common Council for opening of said street or other property, and said Common Council shall proceed to open the same, as provided for in title 6, section 1 to 33, inclusive of city charter. [*Act of* 1867.] Manner of taking private property.

(§ 299.) SEC. 20. The said Board may prescribe regulations for the use of said sewers; may license persons to open the same, and may prescribe a fee for opening and making connection with any sewer, to be paid to City Treasurer, and by him placed to the credit of sewer fund. [*Act of* 1867.] Board to regulate charges for use of sewer

(§ 300.) SEC. 21. Whenever, in the judgment of the Sewer Commissioners, it is necessary for the health or benefit of said city or any part thereof, for any lands or premises lying near or adjacent to any sewer or drain to be drained into such sewer or drain, they shall so determine by a resolution entered on their records, and give notice thereof to the owners, occupant or agent, if known, and if unknown, by publishing such notice in a newspaper in said city one week; whereupon said lands, premises or cellars shall, by the owners, be so drained by connection with such sewer, under the direction of the Sewer Commissioners, within 30 days, and if not done, the Sewer Commissioners may, with the approval of the Common Council, make such drain and connection, and certify the cost thereof to the Assessor from which time such cost shall be a Draining of Pools, Low Lands, &c.

lien on the lands or premises so drained, and the Assessor shall assess the same, and put it into the next tax roll of said city in the sewer tax column, and it shall be enforced, as provided for the general taxes of said city. [*Act of* 1869.]

Board to certify amount of receipts and expenses to the Controller.

(§ 301.) SEC. 22. The Board of Sewer Commissioners shall certify to the Controller, monthly, the amount of moneys received by said Board for permits, and all other matters necessary to the proper auditing of bills incurred by them and the correct keeping of the accounts of the city. [*Act of* 1869.]

INDEX

TO THE

CHARTER

OF THE

CITY OF EAST SAGINAW.

INDEX.

www.ingramcontent.com/pod-product-compliance
Lightning Source LLC
LaVergne TN
LVHW021410110826
845150LV00007B/1858

* 9 7 8 1 4 2 5 5 1 1 3 2 6 *